My Name is Thelma, but I don't know who I am

Jan Malone

ISBN: 1493682172
ISBN-13: 9781493682171

DEDICATION

I would like to dedicate this book to my mother, Thelma McIlwain. She was a great mom, who was strict, but loving. We had chores to do, but also plenty of time for having fun. She gave us deep family roots, but wings to dream big and the confidence to know we could accomplish anything we set out to do or be. This disease robbed her in the end of her personality, but can never take away the memories, and the fact that she was a terrific daughter, sister, wife, mother, grandmother, and friend.

I would also like to thank my husband Al, and sons, Jacob and Keaton. They also endured and sacrificed while I/we cared for my mother.

I must also thank Dick Merrick. Without his leadership of the support group I attended, I am not sure I would have survived the caregiving journey.

A big thanks to all my friends who helped edit, and support my journey of writing this book.

Sincerely,
Jan Malone

My name is Thelma, but I don't know who I am
was written as a labor of love, for those who are caregiving for a loved one with dementia.

This book will help you navigate, and cope with a loved one as they progress through the disease of dementia.

This book will show you a way to keep good records on your loved one. It will also help you assess where your loved one is in the disease process. It will teach you how to handle your frustrations, and give you guidelines on how to find a facility once placement is decided. It will also teach you how to have a meaningful visit.
You will also learn how to you cope with your guilt, and prepare you for the end of life, with hospice planning and funeral arrangements.

Writing this book has been a healing journey for me, and it is my desire for others to learn from my experience.

Sincerely
Jan Malone

Information for the book came from:

The Alzheimer's Association

Google Images

Medicare

Highgate Senior Care

Washington State Medical Association

Columbia Legal Services

Jolene Brakee

Hospice

Table of Content

Chapter 1: What I wish I had known then

Chapter 2: Medical Information

Chapter 3: Medications

Chapter 4: Important phone numbers and addresses

Chapter 5: Calendar legend

Chapter 6: Necessary Documents

Chapter 7: Physicians orders for life sustaining treatment

Chapter 8: **In Case of Emergency** (ICE)

Chapter 9: Laminated Card

Chapter 10: Types of dementia and brain tour

Chapter 11: Global Deterioration Scale

Chapter 12: How to find a facility

Chapter 13: How to have a meaningful visit

Chapter 14: Guilt

Chapter 15: Hospice

Chapter 16: Funeral Planning

Chapter
1

What I Wish I Had
Known Then.

If I only knew then what I know now this journey of dementia might have been a little easier to navigate. This book has been a way for me to honor my mom. Hopefully it will help you if you are caring for someone with dementia. I wrote this book with the intention of sharing information that I have gathered on how to deal with the challenges of caring for a loved one with dementia. As a caregiver there are many things I had to learn through trial and error.

Now that you are coming to terms with the fact that your loved one has memory problems, what does that really mean? Are they in the early stages, and managing most of their daily tasks? Are they declining at a fast pace, and you are worried about their safety, or them being by themselves? See chapter 11 for the *global deterioration scale*. This may be the beginning of many tough questions and situations that you will have to face. This first chapter will tell you a little bit about my journey.

 My dad passed away unexpectedly, and although we knew mom was having memory issues, until his passing we had no idea how bad her memory loss was.

What I wish I knew then, is that it is very common for a spouse to try to cover for their mate and present the situation as being better than it really is.

After a family meeting it was decided that my mom would move to my city and state, to be close to me, and for me to manage her care. My first objective was to find a place where she was treated with dignity and respect. Where she would be given her medications, provided with 3 meals a day, and assist with housekeeping.
I chose an *assisted living facility* that was near my home. See Chapter 12 on how to find a facility. No one has a crystal ball to predict the future, but choosing the facility based entirely on the above objectives was not the right decision.

Mom lived in the *assisted living* four years, but after three years, I began to see the handwriting on the wall. The facility was not secure, and not prepared to handle a patient with dementia. I waited a year before I was finally forced to move her to a *memory care facility*.

What I wish I knew then, was although the facility was capable of taking her to the end of life; they were not a *memory care facility*. I was totally blindsided by what dementia would do to her. It would take a woman who was warm, compassionate, and loving and turn her into someone who was demanding, self-centered, and sometimes downright mean and hateful. Had I done a little more homework on this disease, I would have looked for a *memory care facility* rather than an *assisted living facility*.

What I wish I knew then, is that it would have been much easier to be pro-active by looking for a new facility than being reactive once we were in crisis.

The first year at the *assisted living facility* was a time of adjustment for her. Losing her husband and leaving her home would be a major life event for anyone. She made the adjustments with grace and dignity and it was much easier than any of us would have thought. She had forgotten the details of dad's death, why she moved to Washington, and the time frame in which it had all happened. Looking back now, I realize that was the only good thing about this disease.

One of the first orders of business once she arrived was to line up doctors. I had to reconstruct her medical history, because she could no longer remember the details. (See chapter 2 for the medical spread sheets I devised.) I quickly learned that I did not want to do this every time we went to the doctor. These spread sheets became such a valuable tool for me in caring for her. (See chapter 8)

In the second year, she began losing big chunks of her memory. She called me one morning and asked if I would come over and show her where the laundry room was, and how to operate the washer and dryer. She had been doing her own laundry for over a year, so my reaction was not a positive one. When I went over it was clear that she had stopped doing her laundry several weeks prior. She not only stopped doing laundry, she didn't even realize there was a problem until she had no clean clothes left to wear.

> *What I wish I knew then,* is this is how this disease works. I went over and spent the day helping her get caught back up on laundry. I left feeling confident that she was back on track. However she had progressed to a point of the disease where she was no longer able to retain new information. I did not initially understand that even though she had been doing laundry for years, once she forgot how to do laundry, it became new information to her. Unfortunately I had to learn this lesson more than once, as she forgot basic life skills.

I began to feel extremely manipulated. How was it possible to carry on a normal conversation with her, and the next minute she was unable to remembering basic life skills? It became a habit of hers to call at 10:30 pm telling me she was out of toilet paper, and she needed it RIGHT NOW! In the beginning, I would hop in the car and take a roll over to her. About once a week she would call in distress about not having toilet paper. Trying to be proactive, I started carrying a case of toilet paper in my car. Whenever I stopped by to see her I would check her supply. She got wise to that, and started hiding the toilet paper. As the calls continued, my demeanor got meaner! It took several months, before I got smart enough to leave the reserves in the nurse's office, so that when she called, I could call the facility, and they would deliver the toilet paper to her. Guess what? The toilet paper turned to not having any adult diapers! I didn't understand how a person with dementia could be so manipulative.

> ***What I wish I knew then,*** was that she was not trying to manipulate me, she was most likely very lonely in the evenings missing my dad, and wanting company, and the toilet paper was an excuse to get me to come over.

When we moved her out, she had hidden so much toilet paper that I didn't have to buy any toilet paper for months.

Evening time became increasingly difficult for her. She would tell me wild stories of events that happened at night. (See chapter 9 on sundowner's syndrome.)
She had always been a night person, and there were no activities at the *assisted living* after dinner. She began to dread the evenings. She had never been a big TV watcher, and when she forgot how to use the TV remote, the phone became her best friend. After dinner she would go through her phone book, and start calling anybody and everybody. Sometimes she would even call them more than once! Unfortunately for her family in the mid-west she never remembered the time difference.

She would call me no matter what time of day or night.   Sometimes she would call me a dozen times in the evening, always starting with "I haven't talked to you today".

What I wish I knew then, was that she was experiencing "*sundowner's syndrome*".   This is a typical symptom as they progress in the disease.   See Chapter 9 for detailed information on sundowner's syndrome.

If your loved one is a "wanderer" or not, I would advise you to get them an I.D. bracelet from the Alzheimer's Association or a "Low Jack GPS" tracking device bracelet.   It alerts the person who would find them of the disease, and gives contact information. The Low Jack device looks like a watch and is registered with the police department.   It is a tracking devise should they get lost, that pinpoints their exact location.   I once spent 4 hours at the mall looking for mom.   She was to sit on the bench while I went to get her a drink.   She saw something of interest, and walked off.   By the time we were reunited we were both in a panic.   Don't wait for this to happen to you.   Get identification on them.

As mom's condition got worse so did her paranoia.   She began to hide what she thought were her valuables.   When she couldn't find these items she believed that people were stealing from her.   Mom always had Sunday dinner at our home.
More often than not my husband would be the one that would take her back to her *assisted living* apartment.   Unfortunately he became her primary suspect.   She told anybody that would listen that when my husband would bring her home, he would go through her purse and take all her money.   No one likes to be accused of stealing, and I certainly was not going to tolerate her accusations.   I went over to have a stern talk with her.   I told her that if she didn't stop accusing my husband of stealing, she would no longer be invited over for dinner.   What did I accomplish? *Absolutely nothing!*

> ***What I wish I knew then,*** was scolding her did not solve the problem, in fact, it left me feeling like the mean daughter, and her tears of being sorry did not stop her from continuing to think my husband was stealing from her. The **resolution came when I changed the entire scenario**. Usually while I was cleaning up the kitchen from dinner, my husband would take her home. We switched roles, and once I started taking her back home the stealing stopped. Well not entirely…she then began to tell us that the caregivers of the *assisted living facility* were taking her money, but at least my husband was no longer her target!

It was this stage that I found the most challenging. As a caregiver you want to believe your loved one. Unfortunately, you can't trust that the information they give you is true. We hear so many times in the news about caregiver abuse, and nursing homes accused of patient/elder abuse. So who do you believe? Usually every morning mom and I would talk on the phone. In the beginning she was very quick to pick up on the fact that if she complained about anything I was her advocate and would investigate the issue and get it resolved. One morning during our conversation she told me that she had gone down to have breakfast and that all the food was gone. These facilities are expensive and I was not happy to hear that they had run out of food. When we hung up I immediately jumped in the car and went down to have a talk with the facility administrator. What I learned that morning was that they kept track of the meals that she came down for, and how much food she consumed at each meal. That particular morning she had come down after breakfast hours and the kitchen was closed. They did offer her cereal, but she wanted bacon and eggs.

What I wish I knew then was I could no longer trust that the information she gave me was factual or accurate. I had to learn to not react to her. There were some accusations that I could not ignore (such as the story she told me about her neighbor having a gun) but I had to learn to address my concerns with the facility manager. Many times she had an explanation of exactly what had occurred. (Such as the breakfast incident) If it was a valid complaint the facility manager would work on a resolution.   In the beginning I would tell mom, "You can't cry wolf to me and think that I am going to continue to believe you." Her response, "you aren't here, and they (meaning the facility) only tell you what you want to hear and **I am telling you the truth**." I had to learn to trust my gut instinct, know when to investigate an allegation, and move forward. It was also during this time I had to learn to not argue with her, and **just let her always be right**.

Between her third and fourth year at the *assisted living facility* her cognition dramatically declined. She was losing big chunks of her memory on a daily basis.
My mom was a sweet church going woman and during my youth I rarely heard a swear word come out of her mouth. As she progressed through this disease, she would sometime curse like a sailor.

> ***What I wish I knew then,*** is that your brain stores the *"no no"* *words in a separate area of* your brain. As you begin to lose your vocabulary you begin to pull words from the *"**no no**"* area of your brain.

It was during the time of the third and fourth year, I that was beginning to "wear out". I was still raising my family and working part time.   I am a planner, and I was coming to grips with the fact that no matter how hard I tried, I could not stay ahead of how fast her disease was progressing and what was going to happen next. I was struggling with the knowledge that she needed to be moved to a *memory care facility*. Whenever I would try and talk about making a move she would dig her heals in and say "there was NO WAY she was moving". *See chapter 13 on how to have a meaningful visit.*

> ***What I wish I knew then,*** was how scary this must have been for her. After reading the book "Still Alice" by *Lisa Genova, I realized* that there were times when she realized she was losing her mind, and she must have been terrified. However, she no longer had the verbal skills to tell me how scared she was, and instead her fears were acted out with inappropriate behavior.

When the time came to move her to a *memory care facility,* I worried more about the repercussions that it was going to cause for me rather than how it was going to be for her. She made the move from the *assisted living* to *memory care* with barely a "blip" on the radar. I followed suggestions from author Jolene Brakee on how to make transitions easier for your loved one. I duplicated the setup of her room from the *assisted living* to be identical to her new room in the *memory care facility.*

I made sure that everything was as close as possible to being in the same place. I realized that the room was not shaped the same way, but I made sure to have everything next to her chair, just like it was, or the night stand was on the same side of the bed. And her things were set up exactly as she remembered. I did this to help alleviate her frustration in trying to find things. In the end my worry was unnecessary and she transitioned better than I thought she would.

TIP: *Take a picture of how their room looks. That way you can duplicate it without a lot of extra effort.*

What I wish I knew then was that when a decision of significant importance must be made, **you and your family** need to make them. Discussing it with someone with dementia would like asking a four year old if they want to go to the doctor and get a shot. You need to decide what is best for your loved one and then act on that decision.

During that same time period it was suggested to me I look for a support group. At first I was offended by that suggestion. I was doing the best I could and I had NO time left in my schedule. My husband gently began pushing me in the direction of a support group, and after talking with my pastor I decided that I needed to make time for this. The first group I attended was no more than a "bitch and moan" session to see who could outdo the other person with the crazy behavior of our loved one. I eventually found a support group where we had a time to laugh, information was presented about the disease, and there was a sharing time. As the group continued to meet, we learned from each other. We shared tips and tricks on how to survive being a caregiver. We comforted each other as we talked about:

- Behavioral issues: How to handle situations when you are in public. Carry a bag with a change of clothes for "accidents". What to do if they become violent.

- Care management: When it becomes too much to care for your loved one at home. Coming to grips with placing them in a facility. *See chapter 11 and 12.*

- Medication management: Discussed success/unsuccessfulness with medications. Talked about when is it time to stop all the medications. *See chapter 3.*

- Hospice care: When is it time to consider hospice? What does it mean, and what are the guidelines? *See Chapter 15.*

- Death: The last part of this journey. What to expect, and the feelings that may follow.

This group became an extension of family. It was a safe place to vent and share our "guilty" feelings, to cry, and to laugh, and to be able to walk away refreshed and reassured that we could make it through another week.

During that time I learned many survival tips. My parents taught us that you never lie, and especially not to a parent. One of the survival tips I learned from my friend Bill was something he called *"therapeutic fibbing."* Let me explain. One of the first issues I had with mom is that she wanted to be in control of her money. She felt it was her money and she had done all the family bookkeeping for years. In the beginning we paid bills and managed her accounts as a joint task. The reality was she was no longer acclimated to the days of the week, and didn't remember when it was time to pay bills. Eventually her only request was to have some checks. She wanted to be able to send her grandkids a check and she didn't want to have to ask me for permission for the checkbook. I received a phone call one day from her home church treasurer asking me if mom had had really meant for a check for $50,000 to come to the church. Thank goodness the church treasurer knew me and called me prior to cashing the check.

I had sleepless nights contemplating how I was going to get those checks away from her. I finally bought a check printing program, and printed bogus checks. Years ago they had banked at Crocker Bank, so I put that as the bank name. The account number was all zeroes, but it looked official. One evening while she was down at dinner I snuck into her room and I switched the checks. She never knew the difference. She didn't have any postage stamps, and I did all her mailing, so there was no way those checks were ever going to go anywhere. If there was a real reason for a check I would then write it, and send it as she wished. Of course there would be some serious legal issues if these checks got anywhere. You must be confident that you will always intercept the checks if you are going to try this.

> **What I wish I knew then,** was to follow my gut instincts.
> Better to say NO upfront than to have regrets later.

Another example of "therapeutic fibbing" was: she had forgotten that my dad had passed away. Often when I would come to visit she would ask, "Where is your Dad?" "I haven't seen him in several days"? When I would tell her that he had passed away, she would cry like it had just happened. I learned from author Jolene Brakee you have to get in their time frame. A better response would be to ask, "When is the last time you saw him"? If their response is, "before he left for work, or to go golfing", you get in that same time frame. And then your response could be, "Dad had to work late tonight, so have dinner and go to bed, and tomorrow will be a better day. Or "Dad is having so much fun; they are playing another round of golf. He won't be home until way after dinner". This will hopefully calm their fears and they will have forgotten by the time dinner is over.

I am in no way condoning lying, I am saying you have to think quickly to give a satisfying answer and then be able to move on. Therapeutic fibbing is an avenue to aid in a difficult situation.

One thing that I must point out is just because they have dementia does not mean they are stupid. I was worried about mom having and wearing her wedding ring. She had already misplaced it once, and it took me several days to find the ring. I had also seen other ladies in the *assisted living facility* trading rings with each other. I got the bright idea to find a ring that was similar to hers that was 14 carat gold with a fake diamond. I took her ring for cleaning, and brought her back the fake ring. Needless to say that did not go over well. Even though she couldn't remember many things she knew the difference in the two rings, and she was angry that I had tried to deceive her. Her wedding ring meant so much to her, and I had to accept that is was important for her to wear it. We were fortunate that after this incident she never took her wedding ring off.

In the beginning I also corrected mom anytime she had her facts incorrect. I did that because I thought that would help preserve her memory. Truthfully it also made me mad, when she would tell stories that were mean and hurtful. Many times after a visit when it was time for me to leave, we would both be in tears, or mad. Her pastor would come and visit and he would call me and tell me what an enjoyable time he had with her. I would be crushed, because I could not seem to have that same experience. What I had to learn was that her pastor went to see her with no expectations of the visit, and he had no need to correct what wasn't factual information.

What I wish I knew then, was to never argue with a person with dementia. It is like arguing with a two year old, and you will never win. When somene told me, "Jan, just let your mom always be right", and I put that into practice, my stress and anxiety level dropped drastically.

I had to learn that when I went to visit mom, to go into the visit with no expectations. More often than not, our visits were more like two friends, and not the mother daughter relationship we once shared. When I would prepare for a visit, and keep the visit short, I could usually leave before emotions overcame either one of us. See chapter 13 on how to have a meaningful visit.

What I wish I knew then, was not to go with any expectations of a great visit. Once I started to follow that practice it made it so much easier. I may not have left with warm "fuzzies" about how great a mom I had, but I didn't leave in tears either.

Mom also went through a period of time of being very hateful and mean. She would tell me I was not taking good care of her, and that my dad would be ashamed of me. Or she would talk about another family members and how much she hated them. This was not the mother I knew.

What I wish I knew then, was that it was the disease talking, *not* my mom. I eventually split my mom into two people. There was the mother that I loved and cared for, and the mother that loved and cared for me. I allowed myself to grieve the loss of her. It was the mother who had vascular dementia that I cared for. She looked like my mom, and her voice was that of my mom, but she was not the mother that I loved, she was the woman whom I cared for. I gave myself permission to not have to love the woman she had become. This is still hard for me to admit, but that was my coping mechanism. It was by separating the two that allowed me to be able to leave without feeling sad and guilty when she was hurtful to me.

Since mom's death, my husband and children have become more vocal about their feelings and issues that took place during the time that I cared for my mother.

> ***What I wish I knew then,*** was that there can be fallout residual for up to seven years, and that my family could have benefited from counseling or a support group during my time as a caregiver to my mom.

One of the most difficult days of this entire journey happened when my oldest son was a senior in high school. It was on the occasion of senior awards ceremony night, when the seniors received their honor cords, and were recognized for the scholarships they had been awarded. This was an exciting night for my son, but also one of those monumental moments as a parent. Just as we were walking out the door the phone rang. The *assisted living facility* nurse told me, "your mom is crying uncontrollably and we can't get her to stop, and we need you to come over as soon as possible". I now had to choose. Was it going to be my mom or my son? To this day whenever I think about that night, and the choice I had to make I am still in tears. In the end I chose my son. But to be truthful, what should have been a night of joy and happiness became a night of worry. It was difficult to enjoy the evening and enjoy the celebration. By the time I got to her at the *assisted living facility*, she had written on the walls with lipstick, **HELP ME**. I dissolved into a puddle of tears.

This is a long, difficult journey. Someone once told me, if you have a terminal disease, and you have fought the battle, when you decide to give up you die. In dementia, you no longer remember what things make you happy, and you forget to die. This disease not only can break *you*, but it can also destroy families.

When siblings live far away it is difficult for them to see the decline.   A person with dementia can usually remember a voice of a loved one for a long time. They may present themselves on the phone as being much more alert then they actually are. My mom would tell my sibling that I never came to visit. In the beginning I got a lot of interrogating about why I never went to see mom. I finally started sending emails every time I went and eventually they got the message. Once a month I did send them a copy of the calendar ledger.   (See Chapter 5) You must keep those lines of communication open. When possible try to educate the family members who do not live local about the disease. Hopefully that will solve issues about why the person with dementia acts differently to those who visit, versus those who phone.

Most importantly **TAKE CARE OF YOURSELF.**   Don't allow yourself to become a statistic; many caregivers pre-decease the one they care for. *You really do have choices.* I am reminded of the story about how African hunters capture monkeys. They hollow out the top of a coconut and fill it with rice. The smell of the coconut milk attracts the monkeys and they put their hand in the hole and grab the rice. Once they grab the rice and have their hand in a fist, they can't get their hand out of the hole. They want the rice so badly they won't open their fist, and then they are easily captured. Don't be the monkey with your fist closed. Make time for your annual checkups to both the doctor and dentist. Make sure you let your doctor knows if your stress level is getting out of control. Recognize that you may need medication to help you through this time. It doesn't mean you are a failure, or that you will need it the rest of your life. Get plenty of rest, follow a proper diet, and exercise. Learn to make time for yourself.

What I wish I knew then, was that making time for you is not a selfish behavior, it **is a life saver.** Schedule time every day just for **YOU.** Most of all take some deep breaths, the journey will someday be over, and you will need to be ready to continue with your life without your loved one.

Chapter 2

Medical Information

When my mother came to live in my city, one of my first priorities was getting her set up with new doctors.   At her first doctor appointment, as we started filling out all the "New Patient" information, I was alarmed to learn that she could not recap her medical history. I completed what I could and made a mental note that I would have to fix this. I had physically brought all her medications with me, which was a pain in the neck, but I wanted to make sure to get everything accurate.

That night I sat down at my computer and devised these medical worksheets, so that I would never have to do that again. I always kept them up to date, and kept them in my IN CASE OF EMERGENCY back pack. (see chapter 8)

It became apparent that the doctor's office liked to get all her information in a nice typed packet. The information included other doctors that she saw, along with a current medication list. But where this came in most useful was if we made a trip to the ER. There were many doctors and nurses involved with her care, and they would tell me that they wished everyone would provide patient information like I did. The package included:

    Patient Information document
    Medical Professionals document
    Medical Procedures document
    Medication(s) document
    Important Phone numbers document
    Calendar Ledger document

These forms are all available for download on www.mynameisthelma.org. A portion of the proceeds will go to the non-profit organization HOPE. HOPE is a support group for caregivers of a loved one with dementia

PATIENT INFORMATION

Patient Name:

Date of Birth:

Blood Type:

Drug Allergies:

> Place picture
> of patient in
> this box.

Home Address:

Home Phone: **Cell:**

RESPONSIBLE PERSON:

Name: **Relationship:**

Mailing Address:

Home Phone: **Cell:**

SECONDARY CONTACT PERSON:

Name: **Relationship:**

Mailing Address:

Home Phone: **Cell:**

PATIENT INFORMATION, page 2

MOBILITY ASSISTANCE: (needs help transferring, uses wheelchair, walker or cane)

_____

_____

_____

_____

MEDICAL IMPLANTS: (pacemaker, insulin pump)

_____

_____

_____

_____

MEDICAL DEVICES: (hearing aids, dentures, prosthetics)

_____

_____

_____

_____

Sample

PATIENT INFORMATION

Patient Name: *Thelma J. Watson*

Date of Birth: April, 1901

Blood Type: A+

Drug Allergies: Sulfa, does not tolerate vicoden

Home Address: 1000 Jumiper Lane, Harris MO 60111

Home Phone: 555-123-4567   Cell: 555- 321 -4500

RESPONSIBLE PERSON:

Name: William L Watson   Relationship: husband

Mailing Address: 1000Juniper Lane, Harris MO 60111

Home Phone: 555-123-456   Cell: 555-321-4500

SECONDARY CONTACT PERSON:

Name: Jan Malone   Relationship: daughter

Mailing Address: 1111 Robles Dr. Milan MO 60111

Home Phone: 555-123-5566   Cell: 555-987-6655

PATIENT INFORMATION, page 2

MOBILITY ASSISTANCE: (needs help transferring, uses wheelchair, walker or cane)

Wheelchair – Can walk with assistance

MEDICAL IMPLANTS: (pacemaker, insulin pump)

NONE

MEDICAL DEVICES: (hearing aids, dentures, prosthetics)

Dentures on bottom

COMPLETIN THE MEDICAL PROFESSIONALS INFORMATION FORM:

Complete the *medical professional's information* sheet so that you have all the necessary information regarding each doctor your loved one uses.

This is a handy informational chart. If you need to schedule appointments, contact the doctor, or you need a medication refill, this chart alleviates the need to go searching for phone numbers.

This is also helpful if your loved one is in the hospital, and the hospitalist needs to retrieve information from another doctor.

Remember this form can list all doctors from the Primary Care, to the Dentist, to the Podiatrists.

MEDICAL PROFESSIONALS

Patient Name: _____

DOCTORS NAME	SPECIALITY	ADDRESS	PHONE NUMBER
DOCTORS NAME	SPECIALITY	ADDRESS	PHONE NUMBER
DOCTORS NAME	SPECIALITY	ADDRESS	PHONE NUMBER
DOCTORS NAME	SPECIALITY	ADDRESS	PHONE NUMBER
DOCTORS NAME	SPECIALITY	ADDRESS	PHONE NUMBER
DOCTORS NAME	SPECIALITY	ADDRESS	PHONE NUMBER
DOCTORS NAME	SPECIALITY	ADDRESS	PHONE NUMBER
DOCTORS NAME	SPECIALITY	ADDRESS	PHONE NUMBER

MEDICAL PROFESSIONALS

Patient Name: Thelma J. Watson

DOCTORS NAME	SPECIALITY	ADDRESS	PHONE NUMBER
Morgan Taylor	Internal Medicine	6700 Herndon Ave. Lemoore, CA 98632	(555) 123-4567
DOCTORS NAME	SPECIALITY	ADDRESS	PHONE NUMBER
Keaton Flier	Primary Care Doctor Cardiologist	1300 Main St. Visalia, CA 99661	(666)321-9865
DOCTORS NAME	SPECIALITY	ADDRESS	PHONE NUMBER
Zachary Alexander	Podiatrist	123 Juniper Ln. Fresno, CA 98666	(777)231-9988
DOCTORS NAME	SPECIALITY	ADDRESS	PHONE NUMBER
Jacob McIlwain	Dentist	2255 White St. Lemoore, CA 98632	(555)123-3691
DOCTORS NAME	SPECIALITY	ADDRESS	PHONE NUMBER
DOCTORS NAME	SPECIALITY	ADDRESS	PHONE NUMBER
DOCTORS NAME	SPECIALITY	ADDRESS	PHONE NUMBER
DOCTORS NAME	SPECIALITY	ADDRESS	PHONE NUMBER

COMPLETING THE MEDICAL PROCEDURES FORM

Every time you see a new doctor you are required to complete a *medical history form.* It can become cumbersome to remember all the dates of procedures, the doctors' name, address and medical procedure information.

Once this document is complete be sure to keep it up to date. Whenever you have a new doctor's appointment, print off a copy to take with you. You will be asked to complete a medical history form at the new doctor's office. When completing the patient information medical history, write SEE ATTACHED.

It is also helpful to retain a copy of this along with your medication log. If your loved one is transported to the hospital, the medical professionals need the same information. When you are experiencing stressful conditions, it is difficult to remember all the dates and procedures. This form will help alleviate any missed information.

If you carry this binder with you, you can have multiple copies stashed in the sleeve.

MEDICAL PROCEDURES

Patients Name _____

Date	Procedure	Hospital, City, State	Additional Information
Date	Procedure	Hospital, City, State	Additional Information
Date	Procedure	Hospital, City, State	Additional Information
Date	Procedure	Hospital, City, State	Additional Information
Date	Procedure	Hospital, City, State	Additional Information
Date	Procedure	Hospital, City, State	Additional Information
Date	Procedure		

Sample

MEDICAL PROCEDURES

Date		Procedure		Hospital, City, State		Additional Information - IE info a doctor should know
1925	Procedure	Tonsillectomy	Hospital, City, State	Kansas City MO	Additional Information - IE info a doctor should know	No complications Normal recovery time. No adverse effects to medication.
1950	Procedure	Appendectomy	Hospital, City, State	San Francisco General Hospital San Francisco, CA	Additional Information IE info a doctor should know	Burst appendix. In hospital 1 week. Normal recovery time. No adverse effects to medication.
1952	Procedure	Vaginal birth	Hospital, City, State	San Francisco General Hospital San Francisco, CA	Additional Information IE info a doctor should know	Twin birth. Healthy babies. Normal recovery time
1980	Procedure	Repair broken radius	Hospital, City, State	Stanford Hospital Palo Alto, CA	Additional Information IE info a doctor should know	Plate, pins and screws to repair wrist. Long recovery time, including physical therapy.
1986	Procedure	Angina 2 heart stents	Hospital, City, State	Delta Memorial Hospital Visalia, CA	Additional Information IE info a doctor should know	Successful no further problems with Angina. Normal recovery time.
	Procedure		Hospital, City, State		Additional Information IE info a doctor should know	

Chapter
3

Medications

As a caregiver it is **extremely** important to keep accurate medical records on drug use and make sure the list is updated any time there is a change. All drugs need to be listed, including all over-the- counter drugs. Examples of a *few* over the counter drugs could be vitamins, cold remedies, antihistamines, iron and herbal supplements. Due to possible drug interactions, one drug may play a vital role on how other drugs react. When a medication is discontinued, be sure to write down when and why it was discontinued. This leaves a good paper trail for the future.

Use this chart to list the name of every medication, (it would be a good idea if it is a generic drug to also list the brand name) when the drug should be taken, the purpose of the medication, special instructions e.g. taking the drug on an empty stomach, or with food, the prescribing doctor, and the pharmacy from which it was ordered, along with the RX number.

This spread sheet should be updated every time there is a prescription change, or when a new prescription is added or deleted. Retain all spread sheets in case you need to refer back to them. It is not uncommon for an Emergency Room Doctor to want to add medication. You can use the old document as a reference guide. If a doctor orders a new medication (that is actually an old medication) you have a reference to enable you to tell the doctor why the medication was discontinued.

Keeping this spread sheet up to date at all times also eliminates errors that can occur when providing drug information to paramedics and/or doctors.

To complete this chart, start with the patient's name and date on the top. Any time you update this chart, be sure to put the current date on the form.

You list the medication name either the brand name, generic name or both.

Give the dosage amount.

Note when the drug is to be taken.

State any special instructions for the drug and the purpose of the drug.

List the doctor who prescribed the medication.

List the pharmacy that filled the medications and the RX number.

You can always ask the pharmacist to print an extra label to attach to the medication spread sheet.

MEDICATION NAME	Dosage amount	AM	NOON	PM	BEDTIME	Special instructions & Purpose	DOCTOR	PHARMACY/RX#/Expiration reorder date
Brand								
Generic:								
MEDICATION NAME	Dosage amount	AM	NOON	PM	BEDTIME	Special instructions & Purpose	DOCTOR	PHARMACY/RX#/Expiration reorder date
Brand								
Generic:								
MEDICATION NAME	Dosage amount	AM	NOON	PM	BEDTIME	Special instructions & Purpose	DOCTOR	PHARMACY/RX#/Expiration reorder date
Brand								
Generic:								
MEDICATION NAME	Dosage amount	AM	NOON	PM	BEDTIME	Special instructions & Purpose	DOCTOR	PHARMACY/RX#/Expiration reorder date
Brand								
Generic:								
MEDICATION NAME	Dosage amount	AM	NOON	PM	BEDTIME	Special instructions & Purpose	DOCTOR	PHARMACY/RX#/Expiration reorder date
Brand								
Generic:								
MEDICATION NAME	Dosage amount	AM	NOON	PM	BEDTIME	Special instructions & Purpose	DOCTOR	PHARMACY/RX#/Expiration reorder date
Brand								
Generic:								
MEDICATION NAME	Dosage amount	AM	NOON	PM	BEDTIME	Special instructions & Purpose	DOCTOR	PHARMACY/RX#/Expiration reorder date
Brand								
Generic:								

SAMPLE

Patients Name: Thelma Watson

CURRENT MEDICATION

Date: 3-1-2012

MEDICATION NAME	Dosage amount	AM	NOON	PM	BEDTIME	Special instructions & Purpose	DOCTOR	PHARMACY/RX #/ Expiration reorder date
Brand: *Atenolol*	*1 tablet*	X				*Blood Pressure*	*Dr. Keaton McFly; Fulton Pharmacy*	*RX# 000555 reorder 4-1-2012*
Generic: *Tenormin*	*25 mg*							
MEDICATION NAME	Dosage amount	AM	NOON	PM	BEDTIME	Special instructions & Purpose	DOCTOR	PHARMACY/RX #/ Expiration reorder date
Brand: *Zantac*	*1 Tablet*	X		X		*Acid Reflux*	*Dr. Mark Been Fulton Pharmacy*	*RX# 000555 reorder 4-1-2012*
Generic: *Ranitidine*	*150 mg*							
MEDICATION NAME	Dosage amount	AM	NOON	PM	BEDTIME	Special instructions & Purpose	DOCTOR	PHARMACY/RX #/ Expiration reorder date
Brand: *Trazodone*	*1 or 2 Tablets*				X	*Start with 1 tab increase to 2 if needed. For insomnia*	*Dr. Jill Cascade*	*RX# 000555 NO REFILLS*
Generic:	*50 mg*							
MEDICATION NAME	Dosage amount	AM	NOON	PM	BEDTIME	Special instructions & Purpose	DOCTOR	PHARMACY/RX #/ Expiration reorder date
Brand:	*600 2000 I.U.*	X				*none*	*Dr. Keaton McFly*	*over the counter*
Generic: *Vitamin D3*								
MEDICATION NAME	Dosage amount	AM	NOON	PM	BEDTIME	Special instructions & Purpose	DOCTOR	PHARMACY/RX #/ Expiration reorder date
Brand:	*600 mg + D3*	X		X		*none*	*Dr. Keaton McFly*	*over the counter*
Generic: *Calcium*								
MEDICATION NAME	Dosage amount	AM	NOON	PM	BEDTIME	Special instructions & Purpose	DOCTOR	PHARMACY/RX #/ Expiration reorder date
Brand:								
Generic:								
MEDICATION NAME	Dosage amount	AM	NOON	PM	BEDTIME	Special instructions & Purpose	DOCTOR	PHARMACY/RX #/ Expiration reorder date
Brand:								
Generic:								
MEDICATION NAME	Dosage amount	AM	NOON	PM	BEDTIME	Special instructions & Purpose	DOCTOR	PHARMACY/RX #/ Expiration reorder date
Brand:								
Generic:								

Before filling a prescription you need to inquire about the drug. Don't just rely on the doctor; also ask the pharmacists.

1. Is this drug appropriate for a patient with dementia?
2. Is this drug appropriate for his/her age? There are drugs that should be avoided by people over 55.
3. Does this drug have a "shelf life" in the body, meaning that after taking the drug for a period of time can the drug stop working?
4. Inquire what the active ingredient of the drug is. Then ask if there is a generic drug that has the same active ingredient. If so, will the generic drug do the same job as the brand name drug and at a lower cost?

The cost of drugs, even if you have a prescription plan, can be very expensive. Membership, or big box stores such as Costco with pharmacies are open to **everyone**; you do not need to have a membership to have a drug filled in their pharmacy.

When a new prescription is needed, the doctor will usually phone in the prescription for you if you have all the information that they need. I recommend that you always ask for samples to make sure your patient can tolerate the new drug. I also recommend that if it is going to be a continual drug that you ask for a 30-day supply, plus one refill. If you have a mail order pharmacy option, a secondary prescription can be written for 90-day with three refills. This will allow you some grace time to make sure that your patient is responding to the medication with no adverse side effects before you order a 90-day supply. Ordering a 90-day supply is usually more cost effective.

DISPOSAL OF DRUGS: Do NOT flush unused drugs down the toilet or sink. You can sometimes return unused drugs to your local pharmacy for proper disposal.   If you have unused narcotic drugs, your pharmacist can advise you where you are to take them for disposal.

Finding the right medication for a person with dementia can be challenging. You want them to be calm and not agitated, but you don't want them comatose either. You need to have a good team of doctors. Along with your primary care physician, you need to have a neurologist and a *geriatric psychologist. The neurologist and geriatric psychologist can usually come up with an appropriate diagnosis, and therefore a good "cocktail" of medications. I believe an accurate diagnosis is key in treating a person with dementia.

*A geriatric psychologist is a psychologist that specialized in the elderly.

Chapter
4

Important phone numbers and addresses

IMPORTANT PHONE NUMBERS AND ADDRESSES

I like to be proactive rather than reactive. By completing this document, you will have information readily available.

PERSCRIPTIONS:

When a new prescription is needed the doctor will usually phone in the prescription for you if you have all the information that they need. Be sure to list both a local pharmacy and your mail away pharmacy.

HOSPITAL:

If you live in a bigger city where there is more than one hospital, be sure to state your preference on where you would like your patient transported. Remember to check with your insurance company to make sure your hospital of choice is on your insurance provider list.

MORTUARY:

Even before your loved one passes away, most hospitals and hospice providers will want to know your mortuary preference.

INFORMATION: Rx ~ PHARMACY ~ HOSPITAL ~ MORTUARY

PHARMACY OF CHOICE:

Drug Allergies

City, State and Zip Code:

Phone Number:

MAIL AWAY PHARMACY:

Drug Allergies

City, State and Zip Code:

Phone Number:

HOSPITAL:

City, State, and Zip Code:

Phone Number:

MORTUARY:

City, State and Zip Code:

Phone Number:

Contact Person:

SAMPLE

INFORMATION: Rx ~ PHARMACY ~ HOSPITAL ~ MORTUARY

PHARMACY OF CHOICE: *CVS*

Drug Allergies: *sulfa, cannot tolerate viocoden*

City, State and Zip Code: *123 Main St. Canton, CA 55566*

Phone Number: **555-123-4567**

MAIL AWAY PHARMACY: *MEDCO*

Drug Allergies: *sulfa, cannot tolerate viocoden*

City, State and Zip Code: *2440 Robles Dr. Alexandria VA 66655*

Phone Number: *800-765-4321*

HOSPITAL: *Sacred Heart*

City, State, and Zip Code: *3214 W. Concord Ave. Canton, CA 55566*

Phone Number: *555-765-4321*

MORTUARY: *Baker Mortuary*

City, State and Zip Code: *1212 W. Cascade Blvd. Canton, CA 55566*

Phone Number: **555-666-2121**

Contact Person: *Sarabeth Malone*

Chapter
5

Calendar Legend

Completing the Calendar Legend

I found it helpful to keep a daily calendar of specific events that occurred with my loved one. If nothing happened on any given day there is not a need for an entry. If I noticed something different that caught my attention regarding her behavior or if there was an incident that happened this became my record of events. A calendar is a helpful because you can visually see changes day by day in your loved one. By color coding events, if there are reoccurring problems it will stand out. I would also take a copy to the doctor, to document her month, or to show a decline in cognition, or mood changes. It is a helpful tool when updating family member on your loved ones condition. If your loved one is not in a facility, and you are noticing more and more decline, it can also help you make the decision to place your loved one in a facility. I would recommend putting this in an excel format on your computer (or download from my website) for the ease of record keeping. At the end of each month you can forward your loved ones health diary for the month to anyone who might be interested.

The calendar is a blank calendar, so you will need to add the appropriate ***month***, ***year*** and the ***days***. There is a legend below the calendar that is color coded to an event. If there is something that you want to remember, put the corresponding color on the day it happened. You can always elaborate on the back of the calendar if you feel it necessary. You can also add more colors to record events that you want to document.

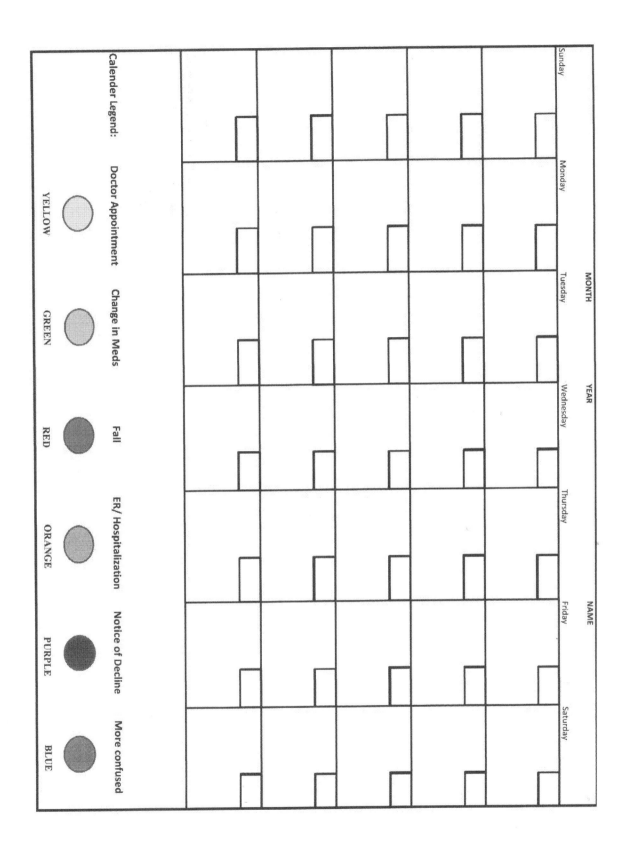

MONTH: May   YEAR: 2009   NAME: Thelma Watson

Sunday	Monday	Tuesday	Wednesday	Thursday	Friday	Saturday
		1	2	3	4 *Crying more often*	5
6	7 *Out to lunch. Good Day!*	8 *Tripp'd over chair*	9	10	11	12
13	14	15	16	17	18	19
20	21	22	23	24	25	26
27	28	29	30	31		

Calender Legend:

SAMPLE

Doctor Appointment	YELLOW
Change in Meds	GREEN
Fall	RED
ER/ Hospitalization	ORANGE
Notice of Decline	PURPLE
More confused	BLUE

Chapter
6

Necessary
Documents

I would recommend that you have several documents in your binder. I would also recommend using copies and **store the originals in a safe place such as a fireproof safe or safe deposit box at the bank.** However, make sure you have access to them as you may need to produce originals in the event something happens after regular business hours.

The documents I recommend that you have copies of are:

Insurance Card

Medicare Card

Prescription Card

Dental Card

Power of Attorney

POLST – Physicians Orders for Life Sustaining Treatment

Health Care Directive

I caution you that if you have copies of the Medicare Card, and or Social Security card in your binder, be sure that the binder is always kept in a safe place, where criminals cannot gain access to confidential information. Your Medicare card number is also the same as your social security number plus an alpha character.

LEGAL DOCUMENTS
Power of Attorney/Guardianships

Power of Attorney: What is a Power of Attorney and why do you need one?

A power of attorney is authorization for someone to act on your behalf. It is a paper that designates to whom you will give this authority. The powers can be limited or they can be very broad. You can authorize your designated "agent" to make health care decisions for you, buy or sell homes for you, and/or manage financial matters. A power of attorney cannot be used to vote in a public election, or to make or alter a will. A power of attorney can be written for a specific period of time, or it can be written to last indefinitely.

Durable Power of Attorney:

For a durable power of attorney to be in effect in the case of dementia it must specifically state, that it will remain in effect even in the event of your becoming mentally incapacitated.

A durable power of attorney must specify what powers are given, and when those power take effect.

A power of attorney can be written to include health care decisions. It will be helpful to have an explanation in writing of what your wishes are, such those involving a living will. You can assign your power of attorney to your spouse, family member or friend, but you cannot assign power or attorney to your doctor or your doctor's employees, or employees of a health care facility in which you reside. Be sure that the person that you are entrusting with your power of attorney is trustworthy.

Specific Power of Attorney:

A specific power of attorney specifically authorizes powers for a specific power and for a specific time frame. An example of that would be: The power to designate someone to work with your insurance benefits during the time you are in the hospital/recovery from a medical procedure. You can also authorize your spouse/partner to sign for you on the sale or purchase of a home. Medicaid is an example of an agency that requires a specific power of attorney.

Power of attorney can be given to more than one person. You can name a second person to take over under specified circumstances, e.g. in the case of death of the first power of attorney recipient.

A lawyer does not need to prepare a power of attorney. However, prior to giving someone one important power, it would be wise to obtain legal advice.

Does a power of attorney need to be notarized?   Yes and No. If you are going to sell property or transfer title, the power of attorney must be notarized.

If no land is involved it is not legally necessary. However, many institutions may doubt the validity of the power of attorney if it has not been notarized. Therefore it is a good practice to have the power of attorney notarized.

Guardianship: What is guardianship, and do I need one.

Guardianship is when the court appoints a person to manage the affairs of a person who is incapacitated. A guardian will usually manage financial affairs because the person has demonstrated the inability to adequately manage their financial affairs or property. A guardian can make all health care decisions, if the person has demonstrated the inability to adequately provide for their personal health and safety.

Guardians are appointed by the court or by judges in response to a petition by the prospective guardian.   First a notice of guardianship must be given to the person identified in the petition. Second, the court must appoint a person ("Guardian ad litem") to make an investigation of the circumstances and report to the court. Third, the guardian ad litem must obtain a statement from a doctor, and fourth, a hearing must be held.
If a person is not totally incapacitated but still needs help, a limited guardianship can be obtained.

Guardians' responsibilities depend on the court ruling. Generally their responsibilities are for the "estate" and the "person". However, a limited guardianship could contain elements from one or both categories.

If you have guardianship of the estate, you are responsible for the person's property and finances. You will need to file an inventory for the court within three months. You will also have to do an annual accounting, and that must meet the courts approval.

If you also have guardianship of the person, you are responsible for their physical, mental and emotional needs. You will also be required to assist with activities of daily living. You will be responsible to prepare a care plan and explain who and how the plan will be implemented. This plan must also be filed with the court within three months, and will be reviewed annually. You are also responsible for giving or withholding medical treatment.

If guardianship is limited the court will decide what decisions may be made by the guardian and which ones are to be made by the person.

If the guardian wants to place the incapacitated person in a nursing home against the person's will, a court order will be required.

Information provided by Columbia Legal Services.

Chapter 7

Physician orders for life sustaining treatment.

Physician Orders for Life-Sustaining Treatment

Last Name - First Name - Middle Initial	**FIRST** follow these orders, **THEN** contact physician, nurse practitioner or PA-C. The POLST is a set of medical orders intended to guide emergency medical treatment for persons with advanced life limiting illness based on their current medical condition and goals. Any section not completed implies full treatment for that section. Everyone shall be treated with dignity and respect.
Date of Birth Last 4 #SSN Gender M F	

Medical Conditions/Patient Goals:	Agency Info/Sticker

A
Check One

CARDIOPULMONARY RESUSCITATION (CPR): Person has no pulse and is not breathing.

☐ CPR/Attempt Resuscitation   ☐ DNAR/Do Not Attempt Resuscitation (Allow Natural Death)

Choosing DNAR will include appropriate comfort measures and may still include the range of treatments below. When not in cardiopulmonary arrest, go to part B.

B
Check One

MEDICAL INTERVENTIONS: Person has pulse and/or is breathing.

☐ **COMFORT MEASURES ONLY** Use medication by any route, positioning, wound care and other measures to relieve pain and suffering. Use oxygen, oral suction and manual treatment of airway obstruction as needed for comfort. **Patient prefers no hospital transfer:** EMS contact medical control to determine if transport indicated to provide adequate comfort.

☐ **LIMITED ADDITIONAL INTERVENTIONS** Includes care described above. Use medical treatment, IV fluids and cardiac monitor as indicated. Do not use intubation or mechanical ventilation. May use less invasive airway support (e.g. CPAP, BiPAP). **Transfer** to hospital if indicated. Avoid intensive care if possible.

☐ **FULL TREATMENT** Includes care described above. Use intubation, advanced airway interventions, mechanical ventilation, and cardioversion as indicated. **Transfer** to hospital if indicated. Includes intensive care.

Additional Orders: (e.g. dialysis, etc.) _____

C

SIGNATURES: The signatures below verify that these orders are consistent with the patient's medical condition, known preferences and best known information. If signed by a surrogate, the patient must be decisionally incapacitated and the person signing is the legal surrogate.

Discussed with:	PRINT — Physician/ARNP/PA-C Name	Phone Number
☐ Patient ☐ Parent of Minor		
☐ Legal Guardian ☐ Health Care Agent (DPOAHC) ☐ Spouse/Other:	**✗** Physician/ARNP/PA-C Signature *(mandatory)*	Date

PRINT — Patient or Legal Surrogate Name		Phone Number
✗ Patient or Legal Surrogate Signature *(mandatory)*		Date

Person has: ☐ Health Care Directive (living will) ☐ Durable Power of Attorney for Health Care ☐ Living Will Registry	**Encourage all advance care planning documents to accompany POLST**

SEND ORIGINAL FORM WITH PERSON WHENEVER TRANSFERRED OR DISCHARGED

Washington **WSMA**
State **Medical**
Association

Other Contact Information (Optional)

Name of Guardian, Surrogate or other Contact Person	Relationship	Phone Number	
Name of Health Care Professional Preparing Form	Preparer Title	Phone Number	Date Prepared

D ADDITIONAL PATIENT PREFERENCES (OPTIONAL)

ANTIBIOTICS:

☐ No antibiotics. Use other measures to relieve symptoms. ☐ Use antibiotics if life can be prolonged.

☐ Determine use or limitation of antibiotics when infection occurs, with comfort as goal.

MEDICALLY ASSISTED NUTRITION:
Always offer food and liquids by mouth if feasible.

☐ Trial period of medically assisted nutrition by tube.
(Goal: _____)

☐ No medically assisted nutrition by tube. ☐ Long-term medically assisted nutrition by tube.

ADDITIONAL ORDERS: (e.g. dialysis, blood products, etc. Attach additional orders if necessary.)

✗ Physician/ARNP/PA-C Signature	Date

DIRECTIONS FOR HEALTH CARE PROFESSIONALS

Completing POLST

- Must be completed by health care professional.
- Should reflect person's current preferences and medical indications. Encourage completion of an advance directive.
- POLST must be signed by a physician/ARNP/PA-C to be valid. Verbal orders are acceptable with follow-up signature by physician/ARNP/PA-C in accordance with facility/community policy.

Using POLST

Any incomplete section of POLST implies full treatment for that section.

This POLST is effective across all settings including hospitals until replaced by new physicians's orders.

The health care professional should inquire about other advance directives. In the event of a conflict, the most recently completed form takes precedence.

SECTION A:
- No defibrillator should be used on a person who has chosen "Do Not Attempt Resuscitation."

SECTION B:
- When comfort cannot be achieved in the current setting, the person, including someone with "Comfort Measures Only," should be transferred to a setting able to provide comfort (e.g., treatment of a hip fracture).

- An IV medication to enhance comfort may be appropriate for a person who has chosen "Comfort Measures Only."

- Treatment of dehydration is a measure which may prolong life. A person who desires IV fluids should indicate "Limited Additional Interventions" or "Full Treatment."

SECTION D:
- Oral fluids and nutrition must always be offered if medically feasible.

Reviewing POLST

This POLST should be reviewed periodically whenever:

(1) The person is transferred from one care setting or care level to another, or

(2) There is a substantial change in the person's health status, or

(3) The person's treatment preferences change.

A person with capacity or the surrogate of a person without capacity, can void the form and request alternative treatment.

To void this form, draw line through "Physician Orders" and write "VOID" in large letters. Any changes require a new POLST.

Review of this POLST Form

Review Date	Reviewer	Location of Review	Review Outcome	
			☐ No Change ☐ Form Voided	☐ New form completed
			☐ No Change ☐ Form Voided	☐ New form completed

The POLST (Physician Orders for Life-Sustaining Treatment) Is currently available in 32 states, and it is an important document to have for you and your loved one. This document is generally used as we age, so our health care wishes are known and what type of treatment measures we desire. This document can *always* be changed as medical conditions improve or deteriorate. The POLST is completed by the physician and the patient or the patient's power of attorney, and then **signed** by the physician and the patient or the patient's power of attorney.

SECTION A: CPR/DNR

You and your loved one will need to decide if they want to attempt CPR (cardiopulmonary resuscitation) if they have no pulse and are not breathing, or if they are a DNR (do not attempt resuscitation – allow a natural death)

SECTION B: MEDICAL INTERVENTIONS

If the person has a pulse and/or is breathing what measures should be implemented?

- *COMFORT MEASURES:* Use medication, give wound care and take measures to relieve pain and suffering. Use oxygen, oral suction and manual treatment of airway as needed for comfort. This also means that the patient prefers no medical transport to hospital unless it is necessary to provide adequate comfort.

- *LIMITED ADDITIONAL INTERVENTIONS:* Includes care described in comfort measurers. Wants the use of IV fluids and cardiac monitoring, but do not intubate or use mechanical breathing. Wants to be transferred to the hospital, but avoid intensive care if possible.

- *FULL TREATMENT:* Includes care as described above. Wants to be intubated and mechanical breathing if necessary. Wants to be transferred to hospital, including intensive care if needed.

SECTION C: SIGNATURES

The POLST document must be signed and dated by the physician and the patient or their power of attorney. Original signatures are required if the POLST is to be honored by the paramedics and hospitalists'.

SECTION D: Additional Patient Preferences (Optional)
You will need to decide if you or your loved one wants to have antibiotics.

- *NO ANTIBIOTICS:* Use medication or other measurers to relieve pain and symptoms.

- *LIMITED ANTIOBIOTICS:* If there is an infection, determine the use or limitation of an antibiotic. Keep comfort as the goal.

- *ANTIOBIOTICS TO PROLONG LIFE:* Use any and all antibiotics if life can be prolonged.

MEDICALLY ASSISTED NUTRITION
Does your loved one want to be tube fed?

- Do you want artificial nutrition by tube or IV?
- Do you want a trial period of artificial nutrition - be specific on how long, and the goal behind the feeding tube.
- Do you want a permanent feeding tube?

ADDITIONAL ORDERS:

- *Be specific about what you want to achieve. What you consider as comfort may not be the same as your doctor or your loved one's definition.*

The POLST document must signed and dated a second time by the Physician.

Once that you have completed the POLST document there are additional considerations:

What do comfort measures mean? What about giving antibiotics for infections or for comfort measures? Is this document honored at all times? These are tough questions, and call for difficult decisions.

When your physician signs this document with the patient and or the power of attorney, have him/her sign **multiple copies**. One copy should stay with the physician in their file, one should stay with the patient, one should be with the power of attorney, and one should be given to a responsible family member or friend. A copy should also be given to your attorney. Without ***original signatures*** the patient's wishes may not be carried out. Paramedics **will** perform life sustaining treatment if there is not a POLST with **original signatures**. I have also learned that airlines may not honor the POLST document. Moreover, I have witnessed the POLST document not being honored in hospitals. So what do you do? Here are some suggestions.

Make sure you have a *health care directive or living will*. This can be used as a legal statement to all your health care providers, and it should state your wishes and desires for *end of life* care. In order to make a health care directive legally binding, you must sign the document in the presence of two adults as witnesses and it should be notarized. This will ensure the validity of the document. Be specific about your desires for treatment: if you want resuscitation, or the use of a ventilator, feeding tubes, as well as hydration state those desires. Give your doctor a copy of your advance directive for his/her medical records. Have your doctor review your wishes and ask him/her if they will honor your wishes. Be aware that a health care directive will not be effective in a medical emergency without a valid POSLT form. If the POLST document does not have original signatures the EMT's are required to provide CPR and other life-sustaining treatments.

Here are some good examples of wording for your advanced directive.

In the event I cannot make my own health care decisions:

- I want my appointed power of attorney to make health care decisions for me, based on the choices I express in this document. If what I would want is not known, then I want decisions to be made in my best interest, based on my values, the contents of this document, and medical information provided by my health care providers.

When I DO NOT Want Life-Sustaining Treatment

- I have lived a long life and I am ready to accept death when it comes. For this reason, if I have or develop a life-threatening condition, I **do not** want any heroic treatment to keep me alive. Even if treatment *might* completely reverse a life-threatening condition and return me to the same health I had before, I DO NOT WANT IT. *OR*

- If I have no quality of life, I consider that worse than death, and I would want to be allowed to die. *OR*

- I do not want treatment if I am unconscious or in a coma during which I do not have the ability to think and communicate, and doctors believe I will probably not recover, or if my unconscious lasts more than (insert number) _____ days.

I do not want treatment if:
- my total dependence is on others for my care because of physical deterioration, *OR*
- pain which cannot be eliminated or can be eliminated only by sedating me so heavily that I cannot converse, *OR*
- if I have irreversible dementia such as Alzheimer's disease.

Temporary life-sustaining treatment:
- I understand it is possible that I might experience an unacceptable quality of life for a period of time when my physician might believe temporary use of life-sustaining treatment would probably restore a quality of life acceptable to me. If so, then:

- I want life-sustaining treatment for up to (insert number) _____ days. *OR*

- I still DO NOT WANT ANY LIFE SUSTAINING TREATMENT.

Be specific about what kind of life sustaining treatments you **do not** want. Examples:
- I only want nutrition and hydration delivered by mouth; if I cannot eat and drink enough to sustain myself I want nothing further. If I continue to linger with no quality of life, I do not want any protein drinks.
- I DO NOT want any surgeries to prolong my life.
- I DO NOT want blood dialysis to clean my blood if my kidneys will never work normally again.
- I DO NOT want transfusions of blood, plasma, blood products, or replacement fluids to replace lost or diseased blood.

Medication:

- I DO NOT want medications if their purpose is to prolong life. i.e. antibiotics, chemotherapy, steroids, medicines to make my heart work and insulin are NOT WANTED. If I am diabetic, I do not want any blood sugar testing. The only medication I request is for pain management.

My wishes concerning comfort care and pain management

- If I appear to be in pain or I am experiencing symptoms such as breathlessness or lack of comfort, I want treatment to relieve my pain and symptoms and make me comfortable, even if my physicians or other medical providers believe this might unintentionally hasten my death, cause drug dependency, or make me unconscious.

Chapter
8

In Case of Emergency
"ICE"

69

ICE In Case of Emergency

Attach Picture Here

Name:

Medications:

Health Concerns:

Emergency Contact:

Name:

Name:

ICE

In Case of Emergency

Name: *Jan Malone*

DOB: *01-01-1901*

Medications: ***see attached***

ALLERGIES: *Sulfa Drugs*

Health Concerns: *dementia, heart disease, 2 stents*

Emergency Contact:

Name: *Jan Malone-daughter*

**Phone #: 555-123-4567
Cell 555-765-4321**

Hospital of Choice:
Sacred Heart Hospital

Name: *Gary Watson- son*

**Phone # :222-321-1234
Cell: 222-321-4567**

Every person in the household should have a backpack for **'In Case of an Emergency"**. This concept was originally planned for families in case of a fire or some type of disaster. I took this concept to another level. I kept an **"In Case of Emergency Bag"** because many times I ended up in the ER in the middle of the night. When I would get a call that my loved one was being transported to the hospital, I grabbed my backpack and was ready to go.

Suggested items for the bag:

Two water bottles

Two juice drinks

Healthy snacks

Book, magazine or word puzzle books

Breath mints and or gum

Kleenex

Notebook with pen

Cash including coins

Cell phone plus an extra battery or phone charger

Something comforting – a bible, a picture, small pillow and or slippers.

Toiletries, brush, tooth brush kit from your dentist, & feminine products.

Important phone numbers in case you cannot use your cell phone, or if your battery drains out.

Chapter 9

Laminated Card

COMPLETE THE LAMINATED CARD

I learned very early on that my loved one became angry if I told anyone that she had dementia. However she was no longer able to communicate accurately with the doctors regarding her medical needs, her medical history, or her current medications.

I devised a 4 x 5 card that I had laminated and I kept in her medical book.

It had the following information:
- The patient's first and last name, and my relationship to the patient.
- A statement that she had vascular dementia and she became agitated if I disclosed that information. The card disclosed she was a good communicator, but that you could not trust that the information that she was giving you would be accurate due to her dementia.
- The card also included my contact information. I usually had several copies that could be handed out, but always retained the laminated one for my book.

LAMINATED CARD

Patient Name:_____

My name is:_____

My relationship to the patient is_____

This patient has (list the disease name)_____

> *She/He can become very agitated when I disclose to a medical professional that she/he has dementia.*
>
> *She/He can communicate, but because of the disease you cannot trust that the information she/he may provide is accurate.*

My contact information:

Home phone:_____

Cell phone:_____

SAMPLE

LAMINATED CARD

Patient Name: Thelma J Watson

My name is: Jan Malone

My relationship to the patient is: Daughter

This patient has (list the disease name)   vascular dementia

She/He can become very agitated when I disclose to a medical professional that she/he has dementia.

She/He can communicate, but because of the disease you cannot trust that the information she/he may provide is accurate.

My contact information:

Home phone: 555-111-2222

Cell phone: 555-222-1111

Chapter 10

Types of Dementia And Brain Tour

Dementia

Dementia is not a term related to a specific disease. It is a descriptive term used for a collection of symptoms that can be caused by a number of disorders that affect the brain. People with dementia usually have significantly impaired intellectual functioning that interferes with normal activities and relationships. They also usually lose their ability to solve problems and maintain emotional control, and they may experience personality changes and behavioral problems such as agitation, delusions, and hallucinations. While memory loss is a common symptom of dementia, memory loss by itself does not mean that a person has dementia. The only certain way to know what type of dementia that a person had is to do a brain autopsy after death.

Alzheimer's disease

1. Alzheimer's disease (AD) is the most common cause of dementia in people aged 65 and older. In most people, symptoms of AD appear after age 60. However, there are some early-onset forms of the disease that may appear as early as age 30. AD usually causes a gradual decline in abilities that usually span seven to ten years. The Alzheimer's Association now believes that the patient usually has AD 20 years prior to being diagnosed. Nearly all brain functions, including memory, movement, language, judgment, and behavior are eventually affected. In the early stages of AD, patients usually experience memory impairment, lapses of judgment, and changes in personality. As the disorder progresses, memory and language problems worsen and the patient begins to have difficulty performing activities of daily living. Examples of this would be things that they have done on a regular basis such as preparing meals, balancing their checkbook and remembering to take their medications. They begin to have difficulty navigating a familiar route. They may become disoriented about places and times. Most people with AD eventually develop symptoms such as aggression, agitation, depression, sleeplessness, and or delusions. They may have delusions that lead to the conclusion that someone is stealing from them or that their spouse is being unfaithful. They may become short-tempered and hostile. They may begin to lose bladder control, and then bowel control. They may even lose the ability to recognize family members and to speak. During the late stages of the disease, patients begin to lose the ability to control motor functions such as walking and may have to be in a wheelchair. In the last stages they may have difficulty swallowing and may need to have their food pureed.

Vascular Dementia

2. Vascular dementia is the second most common cause of dementia, after AD. It accounts for up to 20 percent of all dementias and is caused by brain damage from cardiovascular problems - usually strokes. In some cases a single stroke can damage the brain enough to cause dementia. In many cases, it may coexist with AD. The incidence of vascular dementia increases with age and is similar in men and women. Symptoms of vascular dementia often develop after a stroke. Patients may have a history of high blood pressure, vascular disease, or previous strokes or heart attacks. Vascular dementia may or may not get worse with time, depending on whether the person has additional strokes. Vascular dementia with brain damage to the mid-brain regions may cause cognitive impairment that may look much like AD. Unlike people with AD, people with vascular dementia often maintain their personality and normal levels of emotional responsiveness until the later stages of the disease. Patients with vascular dementia frequently wander at night and often have other problems commonly found in people who have had a stroke. As the disease progresses sudden changes in ability are often apparent. The patient may also suffer with depression and incontinence.

Lewy Body Dementia

3. Lewy body dementia (LBD) is one of the most common types of progressive dementia. LBD usually occurs sporadically, in people with no known family history of the disease. In LBD, cells die in the brain's outer layer, and in parts of the mid-brain. Many of the remaining nerve cells in the mid brain contain abnormal structures called Lewy Bodies that are the hallmark of the disease. Lewy Bodies contain a protein called alpha-synuclein that has been linked to Parkinson's disease and several other disorders. The symptoms of LBD overlap with AD in many ways, and may include memory impairment, poor judgment, and confusion. However, LBD typically also includes visual hallucinations, and in Parkinson's suffers symptoms are shuffling of feet and a flexed posture, which makes them prone to falling. Patients with LBD live an average of seven years after symptoms begin. There is no cure for LBD, and treatments are aimed at controlling the psychiatric symptoms of the disorder. Lewy bodies are often found in the brains of people with Parkinson's and AD. These findings suggest that either LBD is related to these other causes of dementia or that the diseases sometimes coexist in the same person.

Parkinson Disease

4. Parkinson's disease is a chronic, progressive neurological condition, and in its advanced stages, the disease can affect cognitive functioning. Not all people with Parkinson's disease will develop dementia. Dementia due to Parkinson's is also a Lewy body dementia. Symptoms may include tremors, muscle stiffness and speech problems. Reasoning, memory, and judgment are usually also affected.

Frontotemporal Dementia

5. Frontotemporal dementia, sometimes called frontal lobe dementia, (FTD) describes a group of diseases characterized by degeneration of nerve cells - especially those in the frontal and temporal lobes of the brain. Unlike AD, FTD usually does not include formation of amyloid plaques. In many people with FTD, there is an abnormal form of tau protein in the brain, which accumulates into neurofibrillary tangles. This disrupts normal cell activities and may cause the cells to die. Experts believe FTD accounts for two –ten percent of all cases of dementia. Symptoms of FTD usually appear between the ages of 40 and 65. In many cases, people with FTD have a family history of dementia, suggesting that there is a strong genetic factor in the disease. The duration of FTD varies, with some patients declining rapidly over two – three years and others showing only minimal changes for many years. People with FTD live with the disease for an average of five – ten years after diagnosis. Since the frontal and temporal lobes of the brain control judgment and social behavior, patients with FTD often have problems maintaining normal interactions and socialization. Patients steal or exhibit impolite and socially inappropriate behavior, and they may neglect their normal responsibilities. Other common symptoms include loss of speech and language, compulsive or repetitive behavior, increased appetite, and motor problems such as stiffness and balance problems. Memory loss also may occur, although it typically appears late in the disease.

Creutzfeld-Jakob Disease

6. Creutzfeldt-Jakob disease (CJD) is a rare, degenerative, fatal brain disorder that affects about one in every million people per year worldwide. Symptoms usually begin after the age of 60, and most patients die within one year.

Patients with CJD may initially experience problems with muscular coordination, personality changes, impaired memory, judgment, thinking, and impaired vision. Other symptoms may include insomnia and depression. As the illness progresses, mental impairment becomes severe. Patients often go blind. They eventually lose the ability to move and speak, and go into a coma. Pneumonia and other infections often occur in these patients and can lead to death. In recent years, a new type of CJD has been found in Great Britain and several other European countries and the US. The initial symptoms of vCJD are different from those of classic CJD and the disorder typically occurs in younger patients. Research suggests that vCJD may have resulted from human consumption of beef with a disease called bovine spongiform encephalopathy also known as "mad cow disease."

Huntington's disease

7. Huntington's disease (HD) is a hereditary disorder caused by a faulty gene. The children of people with the disorder have a 50 percent chance of inheriting it. The disease causes degeneration in many regions of the brain and spinal cord. Symptoms of HD usually begin when patients are in their 30s or 40s, and the average life expectancy after diagnosis is about 15 years. Cognitive symptoms of HD typically begin with mild personality changes, such as irritability, anxiety, and depression, and progress to severe dementia. Many patients also show psychotic behavior. HD causes involuntary jerky movements of the body, as well as muscle weakness, clumsiness, and difficulty walking.

Sundowners Syndrome

Most of us look forward to evening. There is a transition time from our busy day to the relaxing nature of evening. But for many elderly who suffer from dementia it can be a time of increased memory loss, agitation, and even anger. Family members who care for dementia patients may witness an increase in their symptoms of dementia. It can be painful, frightening, and exhausting for both the patient and the caregiver. Behaviors encountered in "sundowner's syndrome" are often more sever and pronounced and they almost always occur after the sun goes down and natural daylight fades. While one person may express several of the behaviors at the same time, another may exhibit only one of them. Symptoms include rapid mood changes, anger, crying agitation, pacing, fear, depression stubbornness, restlessness and rocking. The more severe the symptoms of sundowner's syndrome are, the more difficult it is to manage patients with dementia. The patient may also put others at risk. They can become physically violent. They may have hallucinations. They may display paranoia. They may also wander off without knowing how to return home. When a patient is "sundowning", they cannot control their behavior.

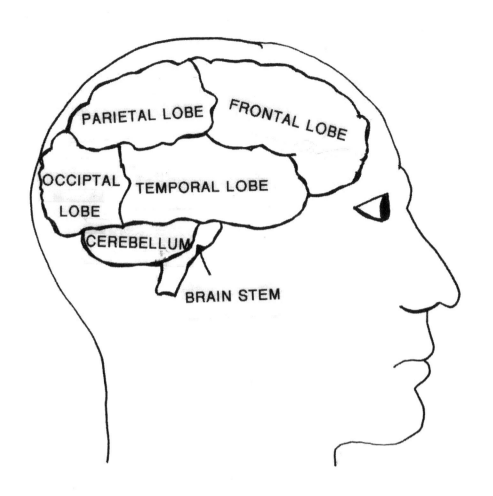

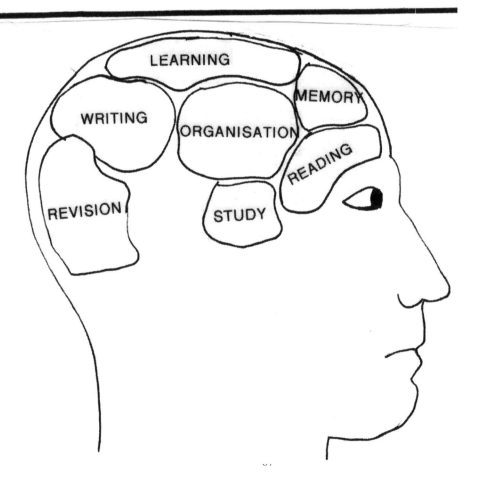

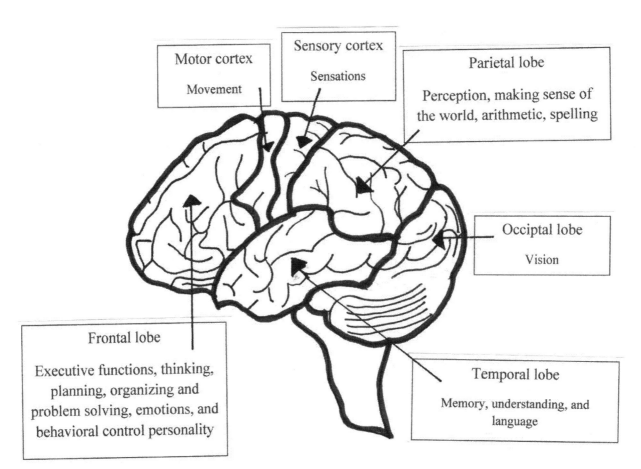

Motor cortex

Movement

Sensory cortex

Sensations

Parietal lobe

Perception, making sense of
the world, arithmetic, spelling

Occiptal lobe

Vision

Frontal lobe

Executive functions, thinking,
planning, organizing and
problem solving, emotions, and
behavioral control personality

Temporal lobe

Memory, understanding, and
language

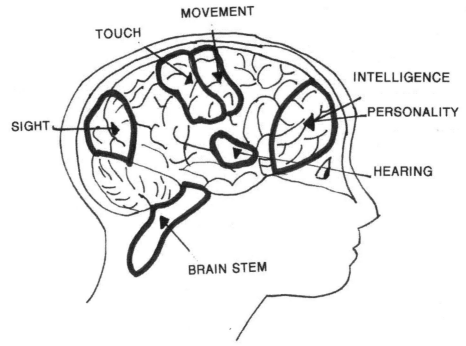

MOVEMENT

TOUCH

INTELLIGENCE

PERSONALITY

SIGHT

HEARING

BRAIN STEM

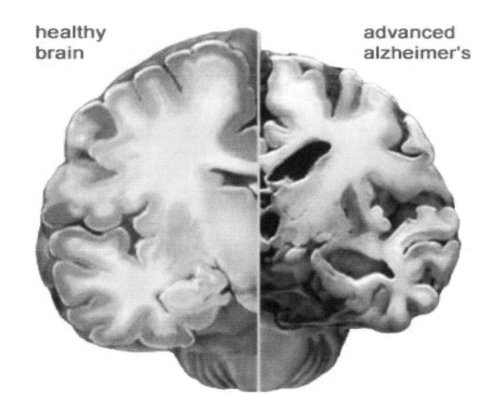

healthy
brain

advanced
alzheimer's

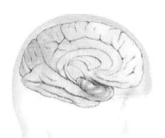 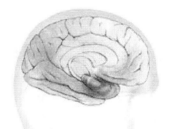 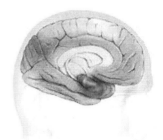

Pre-clinical AD	Mild to Moderate AD	Severe AD

Signs of Dementia

Memory Loss: A common sign of dementia is memory loss. Patients may begin to forget important dates and or events. They may repeat the same statements over and over. Or they may ask the same questions over and over.   They may begin to lose the ability to retain any new information. They may lose the ability to perform tasks that they had known how to do all their life, such as how to use the phone. Giving them a lesson in how to use the phone probably will not work, because this information is now new to them. They begin to rely on family members to do things that they used to be able to handle on their own, such as taking their medication, or doing household chores. They may deny that there is anything "wrong" with their memory.

Problem Solving: Another sign is that they may be experiencing changes in their ability to perform common tasks. Some examples of this may be: keeping track of monthly bills, following the steps or rules of how to play a game, or no longer being able to follow a recipe. Projects may take them longer to complete and may be more difficult to get accomplished. They may also become frustrated more easily when they can't accomplish the task. They may turn that frustration to anger toward the caregiver.

Completing familiar tasks: You may begin to notice that they are having a more difficult time completing routine tasks.   For example, they may not know what article of clothing is acceptable to wear for the season they are in. They may put their pants on first and their underwear over their pants. They may have trouble remembering a familiar driving or walking route. If it has been their job to unload the dishwasher, they may want to do that all the time, even when the dishes in the dishwasher are dirty.

Confusion with place date and time: Another sign maybe no longer knowing the day of the week, month of the year, or season of the year. They may not remember if it is breakfast time, lunch time or dinner time. They may have forgotten that they

Have eaten a meal and complain that they are hungry. They may not know where they are or how they got there. They commonly ask, "What am I supposed to do now"?

Difficulty with perception and visual images. They may begin to have difficulty reading. They may act like they are reading the newspaper or a book, but they may read that same newspaper day after day and not even realize what they are doing. They may begin to struggle with using color and contrast and to judge distance. They may mistake a dark rug on the floor for a hole in the floor. They might pass a mirror and not recognize themselves. This might be due to their not remembering themselves aging. They don't think that mirror image could be them with white hair, when they think they are still in high school.

Difficulty finding words: It may become difficult for them to join or start a conversation. They may repeat themselves over and over. They often struggle with finding the right words or they call things by the wrong name.

Misplacing things: They sometimes begin to place things in unusual places, like putting their wallet in the microwave. They may lose the ability to retrace their steps to find a lost object. When they can't find the missing item they may accuse others of stealing from them, or if they find the item, that someone must have tried to hide it from them. This may get worse as time goes on.

Poor judgment skills: As their decision making abilities gets worse, so do their judgment skills. They may want to give large amounts of money to strangers or charities they never previously supported. They may become argumentative when they are questioned about their memory skills. They may also lose interest in their grooming habits; they may want to wear the same clothes day after day, never wanting to take them off to be washed. Not wanting to bathe, wash their hair, or brush their teeth is very common with dementia sufferers.

Withdrawing from social activities: You may notice that they start to withdraw themselves from social situations, such has going out to dinner with friends. They may stop participating in their hobbies, projects or sports because they no longer remember the steps to follow in their hobby, or the details about their favorite sport. They may withdraw from the activities that they previously found enjoyable because they don't want to embarrass themselves or to draw attention to their lack of memory skills.

Changes in personality and mood: Their mood and personality will most likely change. They may experience confusion, suspicion, depression, anxiousness and fearfulness. Some of these behaviors may be heightened at night with sundowner's syndrome. They may become mean and violent. When they are out of their comfort zone you may notice they are easily upset. As the disease progresses they may become agitated for no known reason.

Simple tests for measuring cognitive impairment

There are a couple of well-known screening tests for dementia. Patients are asked to draw a clock with hands pointed to a specified time – for example 5:30. If the clock is drawn well with 2 hands and all the numbers of the clock are placed in the right order, they have done well. The poorer the clock is drawn the lower their score will be.

Another test is the money change test. This measures the person's ability to perform a simple math task. In the money change test they are given three quarters, seven dimes, and seven nickels and are asked to make change for a dollar. They are given three minutes and, two attempts.

It has been known for some time that the loss of smell is an early warning sign of dementia. The test of smell is to identify the smells of a lemon, strawberry, pineapple, lilac, clove, menthol, smoke, natural gas, soap, and leather. If the participant misidentifies two or more odors they are five times more likely to progress to Alzheimer's disease than those who missed none.

If dementia is suspected, another test may examine specific cognitive abilities: for example, to test language ability, the patient will be asked to name as many items in a category, such as animals, in one minute. Naming fewer than 10 suggests a decrease in mental function. To test the working memory and attention, patients may be asked to count backwards by sevens, or spell a word backwards, or state the months of the year backwards.

To test the reasoning, and ability, they may be asked to describe the similarities and differences between an apple and an orange.

These are test that should be done by a licensed medical professional. The results of these tests can then be compiled and interpreted. The doctor can then make a diagnosis along with a treatment plan.

I often hear, "I can't remember anything, do I have Alzheimer's?" The chart on the following page will help guide you to distinguish between **normal age forgetfulness** versus **mild cognitive impairment** or **dementia**.

Normal Age Related Forgetfulness	Mild Cognitive Impairment	Dementia
Sometimes misplaces keys, eyeglasses, or other items, but can retrace steps to find them.	Frequently misplaces items.	Puts items in inappropriate places. Forgets what an item is used for.
Momentarily forgets and acquaintance's name, but will eventually recall their name.	Frequently forgets people's names and or is slow to recall their names.	May not remember or recognize a person.
Occasionally forgets to run errands.	Begins to forget appointments and important events or occasions.	Loses sense of time. No longer knows the date, year, or season.
Occasionally has to search for a word to use in a sentence.	Has difficulty using the right words.	Begins to lose language skills. May withdraw from social situations.
May forget an event from the past.	May not be able to retain new information. Forgets recent events.	Short terms memory is seriously impaired. Has lost the ability to retain any new information or learn anything new.
When driving may forget where to turn, but quickly orients self.	May become lost more often. May have difficulty understanding and following a map or directions.	Is easily disoriented or lost in familiar places, such as in their own home.
Jokes about memory loss as being a senior moment.	Worries about memory loss. Family and friends notice the lapses.	Has little or no awareness of cognitive problems.

Chapter
11

Global
Deterioration Scale

Global Deterioration Scale

Stage 1:

No impairment (normal function)

Unimpaired individuals experience no memory problems and none are evident to health care professionals during a medical interview.

Stage 2:

Very mild cognitive decline (may be normal age-related changes or earliest signs of dementia.

Individuals may feel that they have memory lapses, especially in forgetting familiar words or names or the location of keys, eyeglasses or other everyday objects. These problems are not evident during a medical examination or apparent to friends, family or co-workers.

Stage 3:

Early-stage dementia can be diagnosed in some, but not all, individuals with these symptoms.

Friends, family or co-workers begin to notice deficiencies. Problems with memory or concentration may be measurable in clinical testing or discernible during a detailed medical interview. Common difficulties include:

- *Takes longer to recall or search for appropriate word(s) noticeable to family or close associates*

- *Decreased ability to remember names when introduced to new people*

- *Performance issues in social or work settings noticeable to family, friends, or co-workers*

- *Reading a passage and retaining little of the material*

- *Losing or misplacing a valuable object*

- *Decline in ability to plan or organize*

Stage 4:

Moderate Cognitive Decline (Mild or early-stage dementia)

At this stage, a careful medical interview detects clear-cut deficiencies in the following areas:

- *Decreased knowledge of recent occasions or current events*

- *Impaired ability to perform challenging mental arithmetic(e.g. to count backwards by 7's)*

- *Decreased capacity to perform complex tasks, such as marketing, planning dinner for guests or paying bills and managing finances*

- *Reduced memory of personal history*

- *The affected individual may seem subdued and withdrawn, especially in socially or mentally challenging situations*

As you start to notice that your loved one has many of the symptoms up to stage 4 and is beginning to show signs of stage 5, this may be a good time to start thinking about placement for your loved one.

Stage 5:

Moderately severe cognitive decline (Moderate or mid-stage dementia)

Major gaps in memory and deficits in cognitive functions emerge. Some assistance with day-to-day activities becomes essential. At this stage individual may:

- *Be unable during a medical interview to recall such important details as their current address, their telephone number or the name of the high school or college from which they graduated*

- *Become confused about where they are or about the day, day of the week or season*

- *Have trouble with less challenging mental arithmetic. (e.g. counting backward from 40 by 4's or 20's by 2's)*

- *Need help choosing proper clothing for the season or the occasion*

- *Usually retain substantial knowledge about themselves and know their own name and the names of their spouse or children*

- *Usually require no assistance with eating or using the toilet; however they may be having some issues with incontinence.*

Stage 6:

Severe cognitive decline (Moderately severe or mid-stage dementia)

Memory difficulties continue to worsen significantly, personality changes may emerge and affected individuals need extensive help with activities of daily living, commonly referred to as ADL's. At this stage individuals may:

- Lose most awareness of recent experience and events as well as of their surroundings

- Recollect their personal history imperfectly, although they generally recall their own name

- Occasionally forget the name of their spouse or primary caregiver but generally can distinguish familiar from unfamiliar faces

- Need help getting dressed properly; without supervision, may make errors as putting pajamas over daytime clothes or shoes on wrong feet

- Experience disruption of their normal sleep/waking cycle

- Need help with handling details of toileting (flushing toilet, wiping, and disposing of tissue properly)

- Have increasing episodes of urinary or fecal incontinence

- Experience significant personality changes and behavioral symptoms, including suspiciousness and delusions (for example, believing that their caregiver is an imposter); hallucinations (seeing or hearing things that are not really there), or compulsive, repetitive behaviors such as hand-wringing or tissue shredding

- Balance and mobility start to become compromised

- Tend to wander and become lost

Stage 7:

Very severe cognitive decline (Severe or late-stage dementia)

- Lose most awareness of recent experience and events as well as of their surroundings

This is the final stage of the disease when individuals lose the ability to respond to their environment, the ability to speak and, ultimately, the ability to control movement.

- *Frequently individuals lose their capacity for recognizable speech, although words or phrases may occasionally be uttered*

- *Individuals need help with eating and toileting. Generally continual incontinence of urine*

- *Individuals lose the ability to walk without assistance, then the ability to sit up without support, the ability to smile and the ability to hold their heads up*

- *Reflexes become abnormal and muscles grow rigid*

- *Individuals become hypersensitive to touch and environment*

- *Swallowing is impaired*

Chapter 12

How to Find a Facility

How to find a facility

Once you have made the decision that it is time to place your loved one, where do you start? Can your loved one live in an assisted living facility, or should they go straight to a memory care center? Should you consider a group home?   It is my belief that if you can find a facility that will offer basic needs all the way to the end of life care, that will alleviate a lot of stress in the future. If you have to continue to move your loved one from one facility to another as they progress through the disease, the confusion for your loved one is enormous, not to mention the stress on you as the caregiver. Placing them in a facility that does it all will take the guesswork out of the need to make a move to a higher level of care. The staff at the facility will be constantly assessing the situation and will make the decisions when a higher care level is needed.

Here is a list of questions that I have compiled from many different sources, which can assist you in making a decision on the right facility for your loved one.

1.   Is the facility currently licensed?
2.   Is a background check a condition of employment for all employees?
3.   Are there policies and procedures to safeguard the residents and their possessions?
4.   Is there ongoing training for staff to learn how to recognize resident abuse, how to deal with aggressive behavior or difficult residents?
5. Are there special services e.g. do they offer rehab services and do they allow hospice to come in?
6. Is there a licensed nurse on staff? How many hours per day? What about nights weekends, and holidays?
7. Is there a doctor on staff?
8. How do they help prevent pressure sores?
9. Does the staff wear uniforms and name tags to distinguish them from visitors?
10.   Do the residents make their own choices about their daily routine e.g. such as when to get up, when to eat, bathe, and when to go to bed?

11. How does the laundry service work?

12. Do the current residents look clean, well groomed and dressed appropriately?

13. How does the facility smell?

14. Do the residents have the same caregivers on a daily basis?

15. Is the staffing different at night, weekends and holidays? What is the ratio of caregivers to patients? Does the ratio decrease when higher care is needed?

16. Is there enough staff to assist with eating if necessary?

17. Does the food smell good? Ask if you can stay and eat a meal.

   TIP: *Ask if the staff eats the food.*

18. Are there plenty of beverages offered?

19. Are nutritious snacks offered during the day and evening?

20. Are records kept on how much food the patient consumes?

21. How often are care management assessments done?

22. How often are the residents weighed?

23. Ask to see a copy of the most current state inspection report. Are there any violations? If so, have they been addressed and cleared?

24. Are the exit signs clearly posted?

25. Are there handrails in the hallway?

26. Are there grab bars in the bathroom?

27. Are there smoke detectors and a sprinkler system?

28. Is the layout easy to navigate?

30. Is the common furniture well maintained? Does it have special upholstery to prevent stains from incontinence?

31. Are the exterior doors locked or coded?

32. Is the resident allowed to bring in personal items/furniture?

33. Tour the facility and stay for a while. **TIP:** *Observe if the staff is interactive, respectful, kind and caring to the patients.*

34. Is the facility open to visiting for family and friends 24/7 or are there visiting hours. Can you bring in a meal for special occasions? Do they have a dining room you can use for special occasions?

35. How do they handle special occasions? Do they decorate for holidays?

36. Does the facility meet your needs for cultural differences? (e.g. food, language and religion)?

37. Are there activities to help keep the residents engaged throughout the day?

38. Are church services offered?

39. Are there planned outings?   Is the bus driver trained? Are procedures in place in case of an emergency?

40. Is there a beauty salon/barber shop on site?

> **TIP**: **Last but not least, not only ask for references, but also ask your friends, your co-workers, and your pastor if they would recommend a facility. Quite often pastors visit many different facilities and will often have great insight about the strengths and weaknesses of a facility.**

It may be difficult to find all these items listed at any one facility. You will have to decide if the facility meets most of your requirements. Follow your "gut" instinct. Even if the facility has met every one of your requirements, but you don't feel good about it, it's probably not the right place for your loved one.

It is not unusual to be making a placement decision in crisis mode. Your loved one is in the hospital and your social worker is giving you a time frame in which you have to make a decision. Here are a couple of things that might help make the decision process easier.

1. When you go for a tour of a facility take a friend or someone who is not emotionally attached. A second set of eyes will look at things differently. You may be so overwhelmed that there doesn't seem to be any place good enough for your loved one, or you may feel so rushed that you can't see the "whole" picture of the facility. That is when a neutral party can help guide you.

2. Ask the social worker at the hospital if he/she knows of a facility that offers respite care. That can "buy" you more time to look at facilities and make a good decision. It may also open a door to a facility that you are considering. It would allow for your loved one to stay there on a temporary basis while you decide if this is a good fit.

3. Once you have made a decision on where to place your loved one, write their biography. Highlight the accomplishments in their life. Include their education, work experience, children, grandchildren and hobbies. Be sure to list the things that are important to them and about them. This will give the caregivers insight regarding your loved one. It will also give them conversation starters as your loved one progresses through the disease.

5. As you move your loved one in, do not bring anything of value. As patients deteriorate in this disease, they may give away cherished items such as their wedding ring, because it no longer means anything to them. Other patients (which we will lovingly call shoppers) may wander into the wrong room, pick out something that they really like, and take it back to their room. Don't be startled if you see someone wearing your loved one's clothes or the other way around. The only person it will bother is you. Labeling clothing will help the caregivers doing laundry return clothes to the correct resident. A source for labels of high quality labels is: www.label-land.com

6. Lastly, there will be a lot of paperwork to complete and most facilities will require a current physical before the resident can move in. Be sure to allow plenty of time for all of that to happen.

Chapter 13

How to have a meaningful visit

Whether your loved one is in a facility or still at home, it can be challenging to have a meaningful conversation and visit. Here are some suggestions:

TIP: Part of visiting is also being observant of the level of care being given.

- If you are going to visit your loved one, make sure that **_YOU_** want to be there and are not going out of obligation. Visit on a day when you are feeling upbeat and positive; this will help set the tone for your visit.

- Make your visit have purpose. If your loved one doesn't drink enough fluids, come in with their favorite drink, stay long enough for them to drink the beverage, and then leave. The mission of the visit is to get them to get more fluids down; and when that is accomplished, it's time to leave. When my kids got old enough to drive, their visits usually started with a stop at McDonalds for 2 apple pies. They would then go to visit Grandma, stay long enough for them to eat their pie and be on their way in 10 minutes. They were her heroes, and she bragged to everyone about her grandsons coming to visit all the time.

- Limit your visits to no more than 15-30 minutes. If you think that the longer you stay the better person you are, you are incorrect. Their brain gets tired quickly. When you overstay your visit, you may find that they become more irritable; and the visit begins to deteriorate. I also found that the longer I stayed, the more deflated I became about my mother's condition. Learn to leave before you become depressed. It is never easy to leave your loved one; but when I had stayed too long, I learned that she was more apt to cry when I left, and then I left with a heaping load of guilt on my shoulders. If your loved one is having an exceptionally good day, that is the time to stay a little longer. Otherwise, remember these 5 things.

- Have a purpose to your visit
- Keep the visit short
- Get in, and get out – leave before the visit deteriorates

- Be done, and leave any feelings of guilt at the door
- Have an escape plan if the visit goes bad. Have the timer set on your phone as a reminder of when to leave, or excuse yourself to the restroom and don't come back.

A question I am often asked is how often should I visit? That is a really a personal decision, and should be based on a few facts.

If your loved one enjoys having you visit, and you enjoy the visit, then go as often as you want. But remember, you still need to have a life. Once your loved one is gone, you will need your other family members and friends so don't spend all your time with your loved one and neglect other people in your life. Your loved one is not going to remember if you were there yesterday or three days ago. Therefore, I recommend going once or twice a week.

How does your loved one react after you have left? Are they depressed the rest of the day or maybe combative? If so, you need to work with the facility and realize it might be better for *them* if you didn't come as often and or stay as long. You might try limiting your visits to once every other week.

There have been occasions where patients react so violently after their loved one visit that they may be asked to refrain from visiting. If this should happen to you, you are going to have to find someone to be your eyes and ears. That may be a good friend or your pastor. It's hard to not take it personally; but you have to take a step back and remember that this is the disease speaking, not your loved one.

How do you have a meaningful conversation with someone with dementia? Here are some tips that I have learned.

Instead of asking your loved one, "How are you doing today?" (You may get a negative response) Try coming in with a positive approach such as: "Hi mom, I am so glad that I am here to visit with you today." Bringing in the special drink can help start a conversation. I also liked to have a hidden treasure in my purse. It was something that I could show her to start a conversation; and even if they are unable to converse back to you, it gives you something to talk about.

I liked to bring in an old belt buckle that belonged to my dad. He had bought it on a trip they had taken to Alaska. Even when she could no longer remember the trip, I could tell her the story of their trip to Alaska and she enjoyed listening to the story over and over. One of the best visits I had with my mom was when I brought in a couple of my Barbie dolls and some of the dresses she had made for them. I talked about how special all the clothes she made for the dolls were to me. While I talked I would dress them and re-dress them, and she sat there with a smile on her face as I recalled a great childhood memory. I don't think she remembered making the clothes, but she saw the joy on my face, which in turn made her happy.

My boys also liked to bring in special things that had been given to them over the years. My dad had gotten them into coin collecting, and so often they would bring the coin collection and explain each coin to her. The good news is that you don't need to have many ideas, because as soon as you walk out the door, they will have forgotten about not only what you brought, but even about your being there. However, **they will never forget how you made them feel**.

<u>TIP</u>: I would often talk to her pastor after he had gone to visit her. He would tell me, "Jan, I had such a good visit today with your mother. She was cheerful and happy to see me." I would be happy to hear that, but my heart would ache, thinking, "Why can't I have a visit like that?" Here is the reason. The pastor went to visit *without any expectations* for the visit. When you can learn to visit without any expectations, your time with your loved one will often be better.

Here are some other ideas of conversation starters

1. Old photos –bring in one at a time to follow the rules above
2. Memorabilia
3. A completed hobby project
4. Tell a special childhood memory
5. Talk about a specific event or person from their wedding day
6. Play a musical instrument for them or bring in a CD with music from their era
7. Follow their lead. If they are talking about a memory let them have the floor. Do NOT correct them if there memory is not correct.

8. Keep the visit as positive as possible

Things to avoid would be:

1. Sad memories
2. Topics they know nothing about e.g., computers
3. Current events
4. Your personal problems (hoping they can help you)
5. Don't ask them if they like the facility, because you will most likely get a negative earful.

When you leave, try to make your departure as happy as possible. If they ask when up are coming back, a good response would be, "As soon as I can". Human touch is so important and is something that is usually lacking. If your love one is in a facility or has lost their spouse, sit close to them during your visit, hold their hand, and be sure to give them a hug when you leave.

However if it is really hard on your loved one, or really hard on you when it is time to leave; don't say goodbye, just excuse yourself and leave.

TIP: If you would like to know who comes and visits your loved one, have a guest book for them to sign. If it is usually the same people over and over, assign them a page with their picture on the page. When visiting they can just add the date of their visit.

Chapter 14

Dealing With Guilt

GUILT

If you are reading this book, I would lay odds that you have experienced this ugly emotion. If your loved one is at home you feel guilty because:

- You don't know how much longer you can take it

- They are driving you crazy, repeating the same things over and over, and asking you the same questions over and over

- They pull the wildest shenanigans and you feel manipulated

- You have been very short-tempered with them

- You can never get anything done because they always need something.

- You are exhausted and dread each new day

If your loved one is in a facility you feel guilty because:

- You feel like you are a failure for not being able to keep them at home

- You're not there visiting them often enough.

- You dread going to visit, because you know they are going to lay a guilt trip on you. They hate the food, no one is nice to them, they are ignored when they ask for help, and nobody ever tells them anything

- They beg you to bring them home or not to leave them, and they cry when you leave

- You aren't there because you are in your own home or out having fun

This list could go on and on, but it has to STOP! Statistics state that 63% of caregivers pre-decease their loved one. Guilt and worry will not change the outcome. You need to put into place coping skills to get through this difficult time. What are those skills? They could be a variety of things. What is most important is to give yourself permission to have a life. When this journey ends, you still need to have relationships with your other loved ones and your friends. You need to hear that it is OK for you to go out to lunch with friends or go on a vacation. Once your loved one is no longer oriented to time, they are not going to know if you have been gone a day or a week. If you get to the breaking point, neither of you is going to benefit from you trying to be the super hero. Make sure that you make time for yourself each day by doing something that you enjoy. Take 30 minutes to read, play a musical instrument, or get some exercise. Put this into your daily schedule as a survival tool for you. Lastly, I believe it is good to belong to a dementia support group. When you are with others who are caregivers, you can share ideas, vent your frustrations, and know that you are not alone on this journey.

There will most likely come a time when you can no longer care for your loved one at home. Recognize the fact that you did your best as long as you could, and now you need help. Many times you will find that your loved one will thrive in their new environment. There will be activities for them to participate in and lots of people with whom they can talk and interact with. When you come to visit, it can now be a happy time. You can concentrate on being the spouse or the son or daughter.

However, your loved one may need some time to adjust to their new environment, and you may be asked not visit for a week or two. When the guilt creeps in, remember these are their rules, and they are for the benefit of your loved one. When you come to visit and they relay all the things that are wrong, listen to them and don't argue with them. Then remember that you did your homework by following the check list in finding a facility, and you know that they are in a safe and secure facility with their needs being met. If they continue to complain, have your escape plan in place, and DO NOT stay.

There are also some patients who become more difficult after a visit from their loved one. They may become violent or refuse to participate in activities. You may be asked by the facility not to visit. If this happens, there are a few things that you can do. Ask a close friend or your pastor to be your eyes and ears. Ask the facility if there is a place to visit from afar to be able to observe them. Be in weekly contact with the administrator of the facility and follow their advice of when you can resume your visits. In the end if it is to upsetting for your loved one to have you visit, you have to come to terms that this is in their best interest. Guilt can easily overtake you on this one, so you have to remember to be focused on what is best for your loved one, not what is best for you.

If you begin noticing changes that you are not comfortable with in your loved one or the facility, don't wait until your next care management meeting. Schedule an appointment with the administrator of the building, or the charge nurse or a social worker; and get it resolved. That will also help you realize that you have done everything you can for your loved one and it will help relieve the guilt.

Dementia can be a long and slow journey. If you are lucky enough to catch this disease in the early stages discuss with your spouse and or parents what their exact wishes are. There seems to be a growing trend that spouses who have placed their loved ones, may get involved in other relationships. Likewise don't be shocked if you're loved one falls in love with someone else at the facility and no longer remember that they are married. An alarming statistic is that facilities such as memory care have a high percentage of sexually transmitted diseases. The residents simply forget about their "true" partners, and sometimes engage in sexual activities with many residents.

If you are still struggling with the guilt, write everything down that you are feeling guilty about. Now address each one of the items. Can you change what you are feeling guilty about? If so, do it; if not, cross it off the list. When you are all done you should no longer have any guilt. You will have changed what you can, and the rest you can shred in your shredder.

If you are still struggling, take my guilt test. Hopefully soon you can find some contentment.

	YES	**NO**
Did you cause your loved one's illness?	___	___
Can you make your loved one better?	___	___
Will worry change the outcome?	___	___
Is your loved one in a safe environment?	___	___
Is your loved one in a warm & dry place?	___	___
Does your loved one have a bed to sleep in?	___	___
Does your loved one have plenty of clothes?	___	___
Does your loved one have plenty of food?	___	___
Does your loved one have to worry about their safety?	___	___
Does your loved one have to worry about finances	___	___
Does your loved one know what day it is or what time it is?	___	___
Does your loved one know the month or season?	___	___
Does your loved one remember if you were there yesterday to visit?	___	___

CONGRATULATIONS!

You are GUILT FREE!

Chapter 15

Hospice Information

When is it time for Hospice Care?

Hospice is an organization that gives a special kind of care for those who are dying. They also offer services to the families of the dying. They offer comfort and support, and they help the patient live out their remaining time as pain free and as comfortable as possible. Hospice is a specialized trained team that cares for the "whole" person. That includes their physical needs, emotional needs, social needs, and their spiritual needs. If you are not Medicare eligible, most likely your insurance will cover hospice care. Hospice treatment should not cost you any extra money, unless you choose to live out your remaining days in a hospice facility. Your doctor or a hospice nurse will have to certify that your loved one is terminally ill and will probably have less than six months to live.

Hospice services may include medication, equipment, supplies, and counseling. Hospice services are not limited to those with cancer, or the elderly. They serve a wide range of diagnoses including dementia. Hospice does not shorten or prolong life or seek to cure an illness. Hospice focus is on comfort and dignity until the end.

So who makes the decisions regarding hospice care? Hopefully you have been working with a team, that includes your physician, a nurse, counselors, a social worker and caregivers. When your loved one is failing to thrive, it may be time to consider a hospice evaluation. Dementia is usually not enough to justify Medicare paying for hospice care. There generally needs to be another underlying condition. (e.g. if they have heart disease and are now refusing to take the medications or if they are refusing to eat and each week are losing weight).

Medicare authorizes hospice care to be given in periods of time. Generally those time periods are for six months. At the start of each period of care the doctor or nurse must recertify that the patient is still terminally ill, and recommend that hospice care needs to be continued. If the patients' health improves at any time during that six months hospice care may be stopped. Be aware that the patient will have to go through the same recertification each new time they start hospice. Many times patients are in and out of hospice three times before they pass away.

Hospice care treatment is not intended to cure a patient's terminal illness. Therefore, prescription drugs for illnesses such as diabetes may not be covered by hospice. If you want your loved one to continue with those types of drugs you will usually not be eligible for hospice. Hospice medication covered by Medicare will be for symptom control or pain relief. In most cases once your loved one is on hospice care they are no longer eligible for emergency room care or ambulance transportation.

There are a lot of "rules" that must be followed to be hospice appropriate, and to stay in the hospice care program. These rules are mandated by Medicare, which is a government agency that pays for hospice care. But I believe there are some major benefits associated with hospice care. If your loved one is in a facility and becomes sick or has a fall, usually the facility protocol will require that the patient be transported to the emergency room. Under hospice care a hospice nurse can be called and will come out to evaluate your loved one. A course of action can be determined without your loved one going to the hospital. When dementia patients end up in the ER or for a hospital stay, it is generally very hard on them. They are in unfamiliar surroundings, and the hospital can be a frightening place for them. This adds stress to the patient, to the caregivers, and family members. There are many services that hospice can provide for your loved one. They can set up bath aids, physical and occupational therapy, social worker services, clergy services, as well as grief loss counseling for you and your family. In the beginning your hospice nurse may only be out once a week; but as your loved one declines, they will be there more often, and in the end they will be there on a daily basis. Once your loved one has passed, someone from hospice will "pronounce" the time of death.

Hospice care can be given at home, a care facility or at a hospice care facility.

Hospice care does not end at death. Hospice offers grief counseling for any and all family members. You will generally receive follow up calls from hospice checking to see how you are coping. In the month of the one year anniversary, Hospice usually holds a remembrance service for those who have passed.

My experience with hospice has been a positive one. The staff and nurses that I have come in contact with have all been extraordinary people.

If you loved one has gone off of hospice care, there is another service to bridge the gap call Palliative Care.

Palliative care is specialized medical care for people with serious illnesses. It focuses on providing patients with relief from the symptoms, pain, and stress of a serious illness. The goal is to improve quality of life for both the patient and the family. Palliative care is provided by a team of doctors, nurses and other specialists who work together with a patient's other doctors to provide an extra layer of support.

Chapter
16

Funeral Planning

FUNERAL ARRANGEMENTS

It has been my experience as a caregiver that I had to learn everything the hard way. This is an emotional time even if all arrangements were made ahead of time.

Making funeral arrangements is never anything that someone looks forward to. It is especially tough if your loved one has not passed yet. However, there are some things, which if done ahead of time, will make your life easier once your loved one has passed.

1. If they are able to communicate, ask them what they would like to wear after their death. Set those clothes aside. Make sure they are washed and pressed or dry cleaned, and ready to go. These clothes should be given to the mortuary staff or sent along with the body. *Do not* dress them in what you want them to wear. Let the staff at the mortuary be responsible for dressing them after they have done their job with the body.

2. If there were pre-arranged funeral plans, be sure to honor them. The mortuary is in the business of making money. Don't become a victim to their trying to upsell you on items.

3. If there were no pre-arranged plans, make sure that a trusted friend or family member can be with you in making arrangements. It is very easy to get caught up in the moment of wanting the BEST of everything for your loved one. Prior to going in to make arrangements, pause to think about what they would have wanted. You also have to be realistic about what you want, and what you can afford; and that might not agree with what the deceased would have wanted.

4. Prices *are negotiable.* The last thing you want to do when making funeral arrangements is haggle about prices. However, if you don't review the estimate, you may be charged for fees that you don't need to pay. Here are some examples:

1. If there is going to be a quick (within a certain number of hours) burial, the body does not need to be embalmed.
2. If at all possible avoid Saturday or Sunday services. Many mortuaries charge extra fees for weekends. The cemeteries can also charge extra for weekend burials. Sometimes these fees are double or triple what you would pay for services during the week. If the weekend is the only option for the service be sure to review the price estimate and see what is negotiable.
3. If transporting the body to the cemetery prior to guests arrival, ask that the body be moved in a utility vehicle rather than a hearse. This can save hundreds of dollars.
4. It would be a good idea, if there is a burial, to ask that a friend stay behind to make sure that the casket is lowered and that nothing is removed from the casket.

If your loved one is living in one state and wants to be buried in another, be sure to make arrangements with your local mortuary. Every state has its own regulations about transporting a body over state lines. Another thing to know is that not all airports will accept bodies. Therefore, your local mortuary will need to make flight arrangements, and the mortuary in the other state will have to make arrangements to pick up the body. All of these arrangements take time and will most likely delay the time frame in which you can hold the funeral.

If your loved one was a veteran, be sure to ask to have an honor guard present. You will then also receive an American flag in recognition of their service. This service is provided for free.

You should write an obituary notice for the newspaper. That can include whether you prefer memorial gifts in lieu of flowers. If memorials are requested, be sure to list the organization and an address.

There is so much to do after your loved one has passed, and one of the most important things is to notify people of the death. Notifying your family is probably a job you will want to do yourself. Having a list of contact information of friends or organizations could be handled by another family member or a close friend. Asking a family member or friend to take and screen all phone calls can also be helpful.

PLEASE CALL THE FOLLOWING PEOPLE TO NOTIFY THEM OF THE DEATH OF: _____

NAME	PHONE #
_____	_____
_____	_____
_____	_____
_____	_____
_____	_____
_____	_____
_____	_____
_____	_____

There will be paper work that has to be completed quickly. Having this information at your fingertips can save time and frustration.

Location of the will_____

Executor of the estate_____

Attorney's name, address and phone number: _____

_____

_____

Bank Information:

Name of Bank	Phone #	Account #	Passwords
_____	_____	_____	_____
_____	_____	_____	_____
_____	_____	_____	_____
_____	_____	_____	_____

Location of Insurance Policies: _____

_____

Life Insurance Policies

Name of Company   Phone #   Policy #

_____   _____ _____

_____   _____ _____

_____   _____ _____

_____   _____ _____

_____   _____ _____

Safe Deposit Box Location: _____

_____

Location of Safe Deposit Box Key: _____

_____

Stock/Bonds/Deeds or other valuable items are located at:

_____

_____

_____

_____

_____

Other organizations that may need to be contacted:

Social Security/Medicare

Retirement/Pension Company(s)

Clubs or Organizations – Such as Fraternities/Sororities

Veterans Administration

Credit Reporting Agency's

Organ or tissue donation. You can donate the brain for Alzheimer's research.
You can also donate medical devices such as pacemakers and hearing aids.

Don't forget to close accounts such as:

The power company

Cable/Internet

Newspapers/magazines

Phone/cell phones

Garbage

Disclaimer: This book was written with suggestions and ideas of how to navigate through caregiving for a person with dementia. The author is not a medical professional and under no circumstances should you take these suggestions as medical advice. If you or your loved one needs medical help please obtain as soon as possible.

Please be sure to visit my website at:

www.mynameisthelma.org

You will find downloads in color for all the medical spread sheets you have seen in the book. There is also a contact place if you would like to leave any comments about the book.

Made in the USA
Charleston, SC
09 January 2014